Understanding Eastern Christianity

UNDERSTANDING EASTERN CHRISTIANITY

GEORGE EVERY

SCM PRESS LTD

334 01730 0

First published 1978

by Dharmaram Publications, Bangalore,
for The Centre for Indian and Inter-religious Studies

First British edition published 1980
by SCM Press Ltd
58 Bloomsbury Street, London WC1

Photoset by Input Typesetting Ltd
and printed in Great Britain by
Richard Clay Ltd, Bungay, Suffolk

Contents

Preface

On 15 September 1977 a 'Centre for Indian and Inter-Religious Studies' was inaugurated in Rome under the auspices of the Carmelites of Mary Immaculate. 1977 happened to be the Fiftieth Anniversary or the Golden Jubilee of the priestly ordination of Professor Joseph Placid Podipara CMI. The happy coincidence suggested to the organizers of the Centre the idea of starting, as part of its yearly programme, a series of lectures in honour of Fr Placid, in appreciation of his work for the cause of Eastern Christian tradition in general and the Eastern Christian tradition of India in particular.

When Father Placid was born in 1899 one era in the history of the Indian Christians of St Thomas had ended and a new one had just dawned. The centuries-long struggle of these Christians, to regain their legitimate oriental autonomy and identity, progressively distorted and mutilated ever since the arrival of the Portuguese in India, had come to a happy close. But there remained the gigantic task of reconstruction and restoration of the pristine unity and identity of the community. During the first decades of the twentieth century, a small band of enthusiastic men started laying the foundation for this task, by a deeper analysis of the past history of the community and the causes of the deep wounds and scars, which still remained for healing and care.

When such attempts were being undertaken young Joseph Placid was undergoing his religious and priestly training in the Congregation of the Carmelites of Mary Immaculate (CMI). He had been not only a keen and studious observer of these developments, but even had occasions for associating himself with them even during his student days, all of which helped to shape his vision for his life-work. After his ordination he spent a few years in Rome for higher studies at a time when, because of the initiative taken by Pope Pius XI, strong measures were being taken by Rome for the restoration of the Oriental Rites and when a number of concerned orientalists engaged themselves in an in-depth study and evaluation of the specific character of the various Oriental Christian traditions and their unique contribution to the universal church. This stay in Rome at this particular juncture, together with his wide reading on matters Eastern and his personal acquaintance with several oriental scholars, sharpened his vision, streamlined his dreams, and provided a clear goal to his mission.

Fr Placid returned home fully prepared to launch on a course of action for the restoration of the identity and unity of the Christians of St Thomas in India. As an eminent professor of theology and oriental studies, an effective public speaker, a versatile scholarly writer, he missed no opportunity for the realization of his dream and the attainment of his goal. For the last twenty-five years he has been living in Rome as Consultant to the Sacred Congregation for Oriental Churches and Professor at the Institute for Oriental Studies. It has enabled him to go even deeper into his studies and researches and to publish a number of books and articles on various aspects of the Indian Church. The latest list of his literary contributions contains some 28 titles of books and booklets, 82 articles published in various papers and magazines, almost all of them dealing with Eastern Christianity in India.

Father Placid is a man with a vision, a man with a cause for which he fought and continues to fight vigorously and consistently, but with infinite patience and dedication that is quite characteristic of a deeply committed person. He has deserved well of his church and has earned a unique place in its history. No wonder then that hundreds of his disciples,

friends and admirers have evinced great enthusiasm, whenever occasions arose to remember him and honour him in
some meaningful way by publishing 'Festschrifts', souvenir
volumes, and so on. Identifying themselves with these senti-
ments, the pioneers of the 'Centre for Indian and Inter-Religious Studies' thought it quite opportune to launch this
annual feature of 'Placid Lectures'. These lectures will, it is
hoped, carry forward the mission and work of Fr Placid. For
they will (1) promote a continuous scientific study of the
Eastern Christian traditions including that of India – their
theologies, liturgies, life-styles and customs, history etc.; (2)
foster a comparative study of the Eastern traditions among
themselves and also between the Eastern and Western traditions so that the relevance of the polarity and complemen-
tarity of each to the overall development of Christian
theology might be seen in clear relief; (3) help the development of an entirely new theological tradition drawing from
the riches of this theology and the Far Eastern (Indian,
Chinese and other) thoughts; (4) provide the stimuli and
opportunities to recognize the signs of the times and rise to
the occasion as they present themselves, so that theology in
the Oriental and Indian traditions may no longer remain
sterile and stagnant, but become fertile and vibrant; (5) in
short further the cause of a theology of the future, holding
fast to the roots, but allowing necessary and sufficient room
for adaptation, assimilation and acculturization.

The first series of lectures delivered in December 1977 by
an eminent orientalist George Every, author of *The Byzantine
Patriarchate* and other scholarly publications, and till very
recently editor of *Eastern Churches Review* is a telling tribute
to the cause Fr Placid stands for. Dr Justin Koyipuram, the
director of the Centre and his collaborators are to be particularly congratulated for organizing these lectures. It gives
us great pleasure and satisfaction to publish them with an
introduction by A. M. Mundadan CMI, himself a research
scholar on the history of Eastern Christianity in India.

Introduction

'Historical causes have divided Christians.' This is the feeling shared not only by people with genuine ecumenical concern but also by persons possessing considerable scholarship. Archbishop Philip Nabaa once told an audience: 'The unhappy division . . . has a number of complex causes arising from the history of the churches themselves, the peoples and their leaders. To understand the great rent in Christendom, we need to realize that Christianity is a deep mystery, divine as well as human, and that creates difficult problems, with doctrinal, psychological, ethnic and political aspects.' Someone else, referring to the difference in outlook between a Western Catholic and an Eastern Orthodox Christian, pointed out that the difference 'is deeply rooted in ecclesiastical and religious history and thought as well'.

There can be no doubt that an important reason for the division between Eastern Christendom and Western Christendom, and among the Eastern churches themselves, is the gross failure in understanding each other. A significant contribution to any serious attempt to bring Christians together again will be an effort to come to grips with the historical causes that have generated and perpetuated divisions. The lectures of George Every, which are published in the present book, shed a good deal of scholarly light on those problems and, therefore, the book is aptly entitled *Understanding Eastern Christianity*.

These lectures which provide a keen historical insight, make a penetrating analysis of the problems arising out of the division in the East as also their causes and thus highlight one glaring fact: In the pre-occupation to safeguard the unity of the Empire, and the unity of faith and observance, both the Imperium and the Christian church failed to give due consideration to the national, cultural, ideological, religious, theological and other differences prevalent among the various groups of Eastern Christians the legitimate pluralism that was characteristic of Eastern churches. The general tendency of the successive despotic governments (Greek, Roman, Byzantine, Arabic) was to create a façade of unity among peoples of different climes and cultures, straightening out the differences as much as possible, even using religious creeds and dogmatic formulations for the purpose. Whenever these governments relaxed their grip, the various elements tended to go apart; and if such a centrifugal tendency was artificially checked division resulted with a vengeance.

On the ecclesiastical level, the East-West relation suffered strains arising from other causes too. The complete alienation of the Eastern churches was at least partially the result of the attempt by the Western church to impose its medieval, feudal concept of the sovereign power of the papacy on the East, which resisted it tenaciously. The estrangement developed into bitter resentment and produced irreconcilable attitudes when the Western church established anomalous Latin Patriarchates in the heart of Eastern Christendom following the anomalous creation by the crusaders of Western kingdoms in Jerusalem, Antioch and Constantinople itself – all territories belonging to the Byzantine Empire and the Eastern Patriarchs.

When one tries to understand the history of Christianity in the East, the following questions inevitably arise. Why did Alexandria and Antioch, both highly Hellenized cities of the Roman Empire, adopt different approaches to the various problems of the divinity and humanity of Jesus Christ, during the fourth and fifth centuries? What made Antioch, finally, to switch over to the Alexandrian theological position, abandoning its own original attitude to the Mesopotamian, or

East Syrians? Why did Coptic Alexandria and Syrian Antioch – both of which had served as bulwarks of the Hellenist interests of the Roman Empire – move away from Christian Byzantium and hail the Muslim Arabs as liberators in the seventh century? What is the explanation for the strange fact that Christians both in Egypt and in Syria-Palestine embraced Islam in huge numbers – Christians who had borne the brunt of Roman imperial persecution for centuries? How can one account for the enduring schism which the Byzantine Church and Roman Church drifted into, even though both the churches adhered to the orthodox doctrines defined in the Councils? Before the eleventh century there had been schisms, e.g., the 'Acacian Schism' (fifth/sixth century), the 'Photian Schism' (ninth century), but they were all temporary and had been healed. Even the eleventh century schism was considered temporary, and several attempts were made to bridge the gaps; the two ecumenical councils – of Lyons II and Florence – proclaimed union with the concurrence of both parties. Why, in spite of all that, did the schism continue and does it still continue now? These posers would help lead an earnest inquirer into a deeper understanding of the complex history of the Eastern Christians, and in this effort Every's insights strewn throughout his lectures provide guidelines for possible answers. I will just pick up, as samples, one or two points the author makes, and highlight them with my own historical, reflections.

One important consideration to be taken into account in any attempt at understanding Eastern Christianity is the phenomenon of diversity and pluralism. From the Eastern Mediterranean Coasts to the Indus Valley there lived, from time immemorial, a wide variety of peoples and cultures; men belonging to different races and tribes, and to various professions, criss-crossed the mainland routes that lay open in this vast area, trading goods and exchanging ideas, sharing ways of life, conquering lands and acquiring power; warriors and merchants, travellers and pilgrims, monks and missionaries rubbed shoulders in this immense sea of peoples.

Whichever people got the upper hand, established their rule over others; dynasties followed dynasties; empires succeeded empires – the Babylonians, the Chaldeans, the Assyrians, the Egyptians, the Parthians, the Greeks, the Persians, the Romans, the Byzantines, the Arabs, the Mongols – all in their turn conquered these territories successively or simultaneously, and ruled the peoples there. As long as the masters were wise enough to recognize and respect the variety and diversity, they succeeded in some measure to keep the complex situation under control; if they failed to do so as was often the case, the various constitutive elements tended to break up and divide, and unity became the first casualty.

Each of the peoples of the Near East with their diverse socio-cultural backgrounds possessed their particular vision of life, their particular world-vision, their particular mentality and attitude, which were partially reflected in their philosophy, religion, art and life-style. Even though certain common patterns emerged in the course of time through continuous interchange of ideas and customs under one regime or another, these did not obliterate the variety to any considerable extent. Take for example Antioch and Alexandria, two cities or two traditions deeply influenced by the Hellenism of the early Christian centuries under the common administration of the Roman Empire. Each had developed particular philosophical frame with which they approached the central core of the Christian message. Their approaches started to differ from each other, perhaps as early as in the third century; this developed into a conflict and came into true lime-light in the fourth and fifth centuries and produced Antiochene 'Dyophysitism' and Alexandrian 'Monophysitism'.

How are these developments to be explained? Hellenism had absorbed different strands and combinations in the early Christian era, and the particular strand that was prevalent in Alexandria was not necessarily the same as the one that gained influence in Antioch. Jewish influence was stronger in Antioch than in Alexandria; moreover, the variety of Judaism that was found in Alexandrian circles was a more sophisticated and more Hellenized one than the Rabbinic brand that prevailed in the Antiochene circles. But much more than all this, what differentiated the christology of Alexandria from that of Antioch was their concept of kingship and view of history. It is the ancient concept of divine kingship of the Egyptians, and their ever recurring cyclic view of time and eternity that shaped the Monophysitic theology, while Antioch was influenced by the Mesopotamian-Syrian concepts of succeeding empires and dynasties which pointed to a down-to-earth kingship, and a linear view of time and history. 'Monophysitism' asserted that the final destiny of humanity was to become divine – one nature with God. 'Dyophysitism' asserted that the final destiny of humanity was to be perfectly obedient to God – to be perfect man. Every remarks: 'The struggle against Monophysitism is a battle for Christian humanism.' What is often called the Antiochene approach in theology is actually the Mesopotamian-Syrian approach. It is interesting to note that the Mesopotamians or the East Syrians became the sole heirs of this approach, though they were least involved in the controversy between the Councils of Nicaea and Chalcedon.

The emergence of the Mesopotamian Christians as autonomous and independent in the course of the fifth century is to be largely attributed to their precarious existence in Pagan Persian Empire at a time when Rome had completely surrendered to Christianity. But their total alienation from Byzantium is also to be understood in the light of the strong-arm policy of the Byzantine emperors: the suppression of the 'School of the Persians' at Edessa in AD 489 by Emperor Zeno, the great attack on the 'Dyophysites' under Justinian I, and the condemnation of Theodore, Ibas and Theodoret in the II Council of Constantinople, AD 553. It was in their anxiety to placate the Monophysite factions within the Empire itself – the Alexandrian, and the Syrian Monophysites – which threatened the unity of the Empire – that the rulers had had recourse to such ruthless measures, as well as to many compromises from the close of the fifth century to the middle of the seventh century: the *Henoticon* of Zeno, AD 480, the *Ekthesis* of Heraclius, AD 638, the *Type* of Constans III, AD 648. But these compromises produced only 'watery' unions. When the Muslim Arabs broke into Egypt and Syria in the third and fourth decades of the seventh century, they found the Copts and the Syrians in rebellion against Byzantium and its Chalcedonian doctrine. They preferred the rule of Mohammedan Arabs to the yoke of Christian Byzantium at least for the time being. Or did they also discover, in course of time, that Islam was only a diluted form of Christianity? Was this partly the reason why so many of them accepted Islam in place of Christianity?

The final causes for the drift between the Byzantine East and the Roman West will remain largely incomprehensible unless we take into account the Caesaro-Papist tendency that had been growing strong in Byzantium and the 'Papal-Caesarism' that was emerging in the Middle Ages in the West. In the East, ever since Constantine turned to Christianity and declared himself 'The Bishop Outside' and was named by his biographer Eusebius, 'A Sort of Universal Bishop', and acted accordingly, not only did emperors interfere in church affairs for good or bad, but the church leaders and theologians gave an honoured place in church polity to the Emperors. Jaroslav Pelikan has rightly observed: 'To be sure, all parties throughout most Byzantine history had high view of his authority. It had been customary to speak of him with honorific titles' and celebrate his authority in Byzantine rituals, liturgy and theology. The iconoclasts raised this authority to a higher level than was customary. Eastern theologians had occasions, especially during the debate over images, for deploring this high regard for the emperor, but they had also reason to remember they owed to the emperor, more precisely the empress, the restoration of the images. Even an ardent orthodox theologian like Maximus the Confessor, did not hesitate to say that apart from Councils or between Councils, disputes were to be referred 'to our most devout emperor and to the most holy patriarchs, the one at Rome and the one at Constantinople'. This was much before the conflict on icons started. Such a role which the Greeks assigned to the emperors provoked Western critics to say that Eastern bishops were venal because this polity made their churches 'tributary' and servile in their dependence on the emperor.

A couple of historical events helped the emergence of papal political leadership in the West from the fifth century onwards. One is the shifting of the imperial capital from Rome to Byzantium. Another, and even more important event, is the destruction of the Western Roman Empire by the Germans and the consequent disappearance of any central authority till the time of Charlemagne. Both these helped the gradual emergence of the special phenomenon which some historians would like to call 'Papal-Caesarism'. After a sort of eclipse for two or three centuries, it started flourishing as reform of papacy began to gain ground in the last quarter of the tenth century under the leadership of the German emperors of the Holy Roman Empire. It grew from strength to strength through the 'Gregorian Reformation' until it climaxed in the pontificate of Innocent III.

The following remark by Every is very significant: 'The organization of Western Europe under the apostolic see was inevitable and natural, but dangerous for Christian unity, because it brought with it a new idea of the relationship of the hierarchy of the church with the kingdom of the world. This was regarded as revolutionary in the Byzantine Empire, where the hierarchy and the government had worked in harmony under the direction of the Emperor. There were also objections from Christians in Muslim lands already being suspected of being Melkites, "the Emperor's men", that worse might happen to them if they served a pope who was the Caliph, spiritual and temporal head of the community of the Christian faithful in the West. These fears were confirmed by the Crusades.'

This and observations which the learned author makes in the appendix, 'Scholasticism' deserve the special attention of ecumenical-minded readers. All the lectures, if read together with Every's other important contribution to Eastern Christian history, *The Byzantine Patriarchate*, can go a long way in promoting an understanding of the Christian East and in paving the way to unity in diversity. Every scores a point in favour of wider ecumenism when he makes the following reflection on Scholasticism.

Latin Christianity, become 'fully articulate, with a theology and spirituality of its own which should be imposed not only on Latins, but on ... Indians and Amerindians ... the Greeks, the Russians and the Copts, who believe that they have superior Christian cultures'. Another view of scholasticism is to consider it 'as a way of learning from non-Christian cultures, from Greek philosophers by way of the Jews and Arabs, who transmitted to the Latins what Syrian Christians had gathered from Babylonians, Greeks, Persians, Indians and Chinese. A return to this tradition in scholastic enquiry led Dominicans to learn from modern psychology, Jesuits like Teilhard de Chardin from the scientific study of primitive man. It has led to enquiries into Hinduism and Buddhism, and into forms of Christian experience, not only on Mount Athos and elsewhere in the Christian East, but in the North and West, where Catholics learn from Protestants and Pentecostalists.'

Christian ecumenism should carefully note the fact that 'there is real difference between schisms in the East, including the Monophysite and Nestorian schisms, and those that happened at the Reformation. The Eastern schisms happened gradually, through a series of misunderstandings about terms, and they will be healed gradually, as Rome comes to understand that she cannot impose her kind of Latin scholasticism as the only standard whereby orthodoxy can be judged.' ... 'All traditional Christians believe that Christ is perfect God and perfect man, so East and West confess together that the Spirit proceeds from the Father and the Son. But the East would distinguish between his temporal mission, his procession of manifestation, and the more mys-

xvii

terious procession of his being, of which all that can be said is that it is from the Father. A like distinction could and should be made between Rome's metropolitan authority in her suburbican dioceses, in her metropolitan province, her patriarchal authority in the West, and her universal primacy.' It is not enough to make this distinction in theory but must be made manifest in action. It should lead the way to the re-recognition, of the 'Pentarchical' or 'multipatriarchal' church polity.

The final lecture on 'The Holy Places' indicates the ecumenical importance of the city of Jerusalem and other Holy Places. 'In Jerusalem and Bethlehem Christian Communions in schism with one another share the use of certain shrines . . .' 'Pilgrims of all nations have never ceased to encounter one another at Jerusalem, and to acquire impressions of one another in that particular and peculiar context . . .' 'Jerusalem has been inter-cultural from the beginning.' Hebrews, Greeks and Latins, Syrians and Armenians, Copts, Ethiopians and Arabs all had and do have their abodes there. Jerusalem is a unique place to bring all Christians together again in unity and diversity.

These reflections may evoke in the mind of the reader the historical visit of Pope Paul VI to the Holy Land in 1964, and his meeting with Athenagoras I. In Jerusalem the Pope exchanged the kiss of peace with the Ecumenical Patriarch Athenagoras I, who later remarked that Jerusalem was a starting point and that he was determined to move on from there. Pope Paul's thoughts on his pilgrimage are particularly significant: 'This will also be a journey of search and hope, the search after all those who are Our sons and brothers in Christ. In the very centre of the Gospel scenes as provided by that blessed land, We cannot fail to ask ourselves: "Where is the integrity of the flock of Christ? Where are the lambs and the sheep of his fold? Are they all here? And those who are missing?" We cannot fail, consequently, to beseech Jesus the Good Shepherd and with His very own words, that there may be but one fold and one Shepherd.'

A. M. MUNDADAN CMI

Eastern Christianity Yesterday and Today

At the beginning of this century the Orthodox Church was in Western eyes bound up with the Russian empire, and often identified with Russian imperial power as Communism is today. In the Russian empire itself, while other religions were grudgingly tolerated, the profession of Orthodox faith was a necessary condition for holding any responsible position under the government, and until 1905 it was unlawful to leave the Orthodox Church for another. Outside Russia the lesser Orthodox nations, Romania, Bulgaria, Serbia, Montenegro and Greece had national churches more or less on the Russian model and closely connected with the state. In so far as they were open to Western influences, Catholic, Protestant and liberal, the position of these was weakened, and they were considered to diverge from Orthodoxy and from Russia at the same time. The Orthodox and Armenian subjects of the Turks looked to Russia for protection, and hoped to be rescued as the Turkish empire fell deeper into decline.

The power of Russia in world affairs had increased for two hundred years and was still increasing, as it is. No one then expected a Communist revolution, although radical changes were evidently coming. Observers of Russian affairs were generally impressed by the renewal of interest there in art and literature, philosophy and religion. The Russian intelligentsia were no longer negative, as they had been twenty years earlier, in their attitude to popular folklore and traditions preserved by the peasants who had not shared in

1

the enlightenment that came to Russia with Peter the Great. They wanted to go to the people and to share their way of life, as others did afterwards in India. This renaissance of Russian culture[1] was making all Russians more aware of the distinctive character of their own religious tradition, of differences between Eastern Orthodoxy and Western Catholicism and Protestantism. On the other hand it might be expected that the coming of religious freedom would lead to a separation of church and state, or at any rate of the church's synod and the machinery of imperial government.[2] This would lead to a reconsideration of the how and why of the schism between East and West, and perhaps in the long run to their reconciliation.

If the Russian empire had been reformed but remained intact, with an element of representative government in the institutions of church and state, Russian influence would certainly have increased, not only in the smaller Orthodox nations, but among all her neighbours. In 1908 the Turkish empire had long been in decline and its final dissolution seemed to be beginning with the Young Turk revolution, the Austrian annexation of Bosnia and Herzgovina, and Bulgaria's declaration of independence. France, and more recently Britain, had given up the idea of protecting Turkey against Russia, and both had begun to stake claims for spheres of influence in Syria. In 1907 Russia and Britain had agreed on the definition of their spheres in Persia. In 1913 during the Balkan wars between Turkey and Russia's allies, Italy, an ally of Germany and Austria, laid hold of Libya, an outlying Turkish possession. It was not impossible that Germany as well as Italy might be drawn into agreement with Britain, France and Russia over spheres of influence in the Turkish empire. But to Austria-Hungary the rapid collapse of Turkey brought imminent danger. The victories of Serbia, not only over Turkey but over Bulgaria when it came to the division of the Macedonian spoils, enhanced the prestige of the Karageorgevitch dynasty, who had always been loyal to Russia, and the attraction of their Serbia not only for the

Orthodox but for other discontented Southern Slavs in Austria-Hungary, for Slovenes, Dalmatians and Croats, who were and are Catholics. Something would have to be done to meet their grievances, but only after Serbia had been humiliated and her rulers eliminated from the scene. An occasion for this was provided by the assassination of the heir to the Austrian throne by a Slav terrorist at Serajevo in Bosnia. The bomb was traced to Serbia. In a punitive war between Serbia and Austria-Hungary Russia could not be neutral, nor could Germany in a war between Russia and Austria.

In retrospect we now see that the war of 1914 was a disaster for all the combatants and for Europe. But at the time both sides believed that they fought to save civilization. That the end of the Turkish empire would be precipitated was taken for granted, but no one expected that the Turks, having lost their dependencies, would succeed in enlarging their living space by expelling the Armenians from most of Armenia, and the Greeks from cities in Asia that were Greek long before the Christian era. If the Triple Entente had won the war with Russia intact Armenia would have come under Russian protection Syria and Cilicia under French, Palestine and Mesopotamia under British. Some international agreement would have been made about Constantinople and the Dardanelles, to the advantage of Greek Christians there and of the Orthodox in Palestine. If Germany and Austria had defeated France as well as Russia, and brought Britain to an agreement before the complete collapse of the Russian empire, the practical result might well have been in substance much the same. The Greeks of Smyrna and Constantinople, and the Armenians, would have come under Austrian, not Russian protection, but this would have increased their sense of solidarity with the Russians as Orthodox Eastern Christians united in fear of the encroachments of Rome. Saint Sophia and the mosques of Constantinople would not have been museums, and some of them might have been restored to the Christians to strengthen the hands of the Patriarchs of

Constantinople, Antioch[3] and Jerusalem in their dealings with the influx of Russian pilgrims who had much influence with the Arab Orthodox in Syria and Palestine. There Britain, and probably France, would have retained spheres of influence, even if the German sphere extended from Berlin to Baghdad.

But Russia fell before Austria-Hungary, and even before Turkey. The influx of pilgrims was followed by the flight of exiles in large numbers to the holy places, where Russian plans for building new schools and churches were interrupted by the war and never resumed. At first the exiles had hopes of return in a short time, but after 1921 they had no serious expectation of help from the Western powers. They fell into two classes: those who came out with the White armies were and continued to be fighting royalists. They had lost the civil war, but in their eyes the old was the real Russia. The revolution was in February, not October, 1917, and the slide to doom in church and state began in 1905–6. They were unwilling to associate with anyone who had served in the provisional government or played a part in persuading the Tsar to abdicate.[4] Those who remained in Russia were in their eyes victims, dupes or traitors. They had no authority to speak for the church or for the nation.

The exiles who set up a synod for 'the Russian Orthodox Church abroad' were firm in their allegiance to church and empire. They would make no concessions to the revolution or to Western heresy and schism, but live apart and bring up their children in the memory of a lost land of promise. They did not and do not deny the existence of Christians in Russia, but because no organization there can function in freedom, they deny that the church in Russia can have any organization at all that is not a façade set up by the new rulers for their own purposes. In this way they have encouraged an impression that Christians in Russia are ready and waiting for missionaries to convert them to other forms of Christian belief, for smuggled Bibles and secret Masses offered in underground sanctuaries. The success of the Baptists has done something to confirm this, and to diffuse the idea that Orthodoxy has gone with the old order, and that Orthodox Christians are ready to become Christians of another kind, not only in Russia and in other countries now controlled by the Communists, but in the emigration. The hard line taken by the White Russian exiles cannot be expected to hold their great grandchildren to the third and fourth generation. Even Greeks of the dispersion, who have also a hard line, are affected by the cultures of the lands in which they have come to live. American Greeks send their children to Catholic schools and wish to worship, like Roman Catholics, in the English language.

But as there was and is a Greek dispersion all over the world, so there was a Russian dispersion before 1917. There was a Russian emigration in France, and especially in Paris, in the nineteenth century. Some of this was wealthy and loyal to the Russian government, anxious only to escape from the physical rigours of the Russian climate. Others were exiles, critical of the administration of the church as well as of the state, but these were patriots, sick for their homeland, often much more devoted to Russian traditions than were aristocrats living abroad. Those who ministered at the Russian church in the rue Daru in Paris were aware of this and alive to their needs. Paris became a natural centre for those who left Russia in the 1920s as it became more and more difficult for anyone to hold down a teaching job who did not conform to Marx-Leninist orthodoxy. This was another kind of emigration. Some of its members indeed had come out in the wake of the White armies, because the accidents of the civil war had set them on the White side of the line, but Russian intellectuals did not share the royalist view of the Russian Revolution, in whose first and second stages they had participated. They were hostile to the Bolsheviks, but not to those who had stayed behind and accepted their rule. Many of them had stayed themselves as long as they could.

The Metropolitan Eulogius had been put in charge of the Russian parishes in Western Europe by the Patriarch Tikhon of Moscow. In 1922 he moved his headquarters from Berlin to Paris, where he made the church in the rue Daru his cathedral, and began to take steps for the establishment of a Russian theological institute in the rue de Crimée in Botzaris.[5] This became a rallying point for theologians, historians and philosophers, and a place where students could be trained to serve in the priesthood in the emigration or in Russia, as circumstances might require. Eulogius and his friends continued to maintain what contact they could with the little that was left of patriarchal organization in Russia itself. This brought them into conflict with most of the other bishops in exile, who set up a synod for 'the Russian Church Abroad' and claimed to be all that was left of it. This came to a head when in 1927 the Metropolitan Sergius, who was acting as *locum–tenens* for the Moscow Patriarchate, vacant since the death in prison of the Patriarch Tikhon, took an oath of fidelity to the Soviet government, and required the clergy of his obedience to do the same. In correspondence with the Metropolitan Eulogius[6] he allowed that clergy in the emigration, who were not Soviet citizens, could interpret the oath he had taken as imposing upon them an obligation 'not to use the pulpit as a political platform'. In this sense Eulogius and his friends accepted the oath and remained subjects of Sergius, while the bishops of 'the Russian Church Abroad' denounced it and henceforth declared that Sergius was simply a stooge of the Communists.

Three years later however Sergius himself broke with Eulogius, who had appeared on a platform in London with Anglicans and others protesting against religious persecution. He preferred not to be involved in what might happen at the Institute of Saint-Serge, before the eyes of the Paris press and of reporters from the Soviet Union. Eulogius commended himself to the Patriarch of Constantinople, Photius, who claimed responsibility for all the dispersed Orthodox. In this he was followed by the professors and students of Saint-Serge, but some others in Paris who were critical of this maintained a parish in obedience to the Moscow Patriarchate at least in theory, despite the practical difficulty of communicating with Sergius.

So a threefold division in the Russian emigration developed, which has continued for half a century on much the same lines. The reasons for this took time to become plain. It is obvious that Christians in Soviet Russia could not afford to be identified with propaganda against the Soviet government, but they made a distinction between the 'Russian Church Abroad' and those in the emigration who are not identified with the hard line that denies the possibility of any genuine ecclesiastical organization in the Soviet Union. This became clearer later when Russians in America, who have the same kind of attitude to their ancestral inheritance as Irish, Polish and Italian Catholics, and German Catholics and Protestants, became involved in plans for an American Orthodox Church. No doubt the Soviet government has its own reasons for favouring anything that would detach American Orthodox from political groups that work for a counter-revolution, not only in Russia but in Romania, Bulgaria and Serbia. But the Orthodox in Russia have reasons of their own for favouring the development of institutions in America on the lines of the Institute of Saint-Serge in Paris, where Russian theological thought can develop in freedom. In Western Europe there are still divisions between those who retain their allegiance to the Moscow Patriarchate and those who do not, while still remaining distinct from the 'Russian Church Abroad'. But in America the movement towards an American Orthodox Church has been encouraged by Moscow, but not by the Patriarchate of Constantinople, which has become very dependent on the Greek dispersion for material support. Some of the most prosperous Greeks, as we might expect, are Americans, who in the modern as in the ancient world desire to retain their Greek culture and connections.

All the Orthodox churches, not only those in the emigration, were in need of help from Western Christians in the years between the two world wars. Serbia, Bulgaria and

Romania had suffered much and were still suffering from the consequences of the war and of the Russian revolution. Syrian and Armenian Christians were suffering from the loss of Russian help and of Russian funds. The Holy Places were full of emigrés where there had been pilgrims with rich offerings. Catholic help was readily available, but there was a natural reluctance to depend upon it, for fear that the acceptance of charity would lead the next generation into Eastern churches in communion with Rome. At this time the Ecumenical Movement was in process of formation. The Anglicans involved, many of whom were accustomed to regard Eastern Orthodoxy as the best available representation in the modern world of the undivided church of the Fathers and the early Ecumenical Councils, were eager to persuade Protestants that in considering the proper basis for faith and order in the coming Great Church of the future they ought to take the Orthodox into consideration. If the Greeks in Constantinople, Alexandria and Jerusalem as well as in Greece and Cyprus, the Romanians and the southern Slavs in Serbia and Bulgaria were accessible as the church in Russia was not, the theologians of the Russian emigration were more articulate, and had some claim to speak for the silent majority of the Russian people. Those in Paris had contacts with the American YMCA, whose leader, John R. Mott, was one of the driving forces behind the Ecumenical Movement.[7] At World Conferences of Christians between the two wars, at Stockholm in 1925, at Lausanne in 1928, and at Oxford and Edinburgh in 1937, the Orthodox presence made the movement more than Protestant. Without it, despite some Anglican protests, it would have been Pan-Protestant and probably too Liberal Protestant to give room for the renewal of Protestant orthodoxy in the dialectical theology of Karl Barth. What was large enough for such Russian Orthodox theologians as Leo Zander and Georges Florovsky had a place for Barth as well as for Anglo-Catholics such as Michael Ramsey, and a prospect of a place for interested Roman Catholics.

That the Orthodox were in at the beginning was partly, but not entirely, a consequence of their difficult material situation. They had always taken account, at least in theory, of the possibility of an authentic church life outside their own communion. Rome had become more negative about this since the Reformation, but those Catholics who made a positive approach to the Ecumenical Movement saw the Orthodox in it as speaking for them. The presence of theologians of the emigration made the Orthodox representation in the movement more Russian than Greek. If this aroused suspicions among evangelical Protestants, it also convinced many Catholics that the Russian emigration was open to unorthodox influences, Anglican and liberal Protestant. Some Anglicans in the Anglo-Catholic tradition shared these doubts, believing that reunion movements begin in evangelical pietism and end in liberalism. They are no way to the union of Christendom, which can only come through corporate submission to the Roman See.

There were other Catholics however whose interest in the renewal of Russian Orthodoxy began with developments in Russia before 1914 and before the beginning of the century. They saw in Vladimir Soloviev a Russian Newman, who like Newman had left behind him an influence in his own church and nation, both in Russia and in the emigration. Soloviev was a prophet of reunion between Russia and Rome. Unlike Newman in this, he came to believe that the Orthodox Church and the Roman Catholic Church were in truth one, that the division between them was a wound within the one body and could be healed by reconciliation. Neither was complete without the other. There was therefore some ambiguity about his final position. He received his communion from a Catholic priest, but never left the Orthodox Church, where he was given communion at the end of his life. Anglicans before and after Newman have taken a similar view of the schism between the Church of England and Rome, but this is difficult to sustain, and if Newman ever held it, he soon gave it up. Soloviev's view of the schism between East and West has since been confirmed by historical research, at least in the sense that no one can draw a definite line after which a schism that could be healed became a definite separation into distinct bodies both claiming to be the whole church.[8] Western Catholics in the Middle Ages generally regarded the Eastern churches as unruly and rebellious members of the one Catholic Church. The Orthodox at this time and afterwards[9] continued to acknowledge the primacy of Rome. Their doubts were of Rome's orthodoxy in the doctrine of the trinity and in other, lesser matters, but they were obliged to agree that the Western churches 'had never been condemned synodically'. A synod without Rome would not be ecumenical. The most that all could agree to say was that the Western churches 'had become alien from the other patriarchates',[10] the ancient centres of the church at Alexandria and Antioch, Constantinople and Jerusalem. On the Western side however communion with Rome became the essential test of Catholic communion, to be applied to every schism.

Roman Catholics who applied it in the 1920s were quite certain that the Eastern Orthodox were in schism, and that those of them who were involved in the Ecumenical Movement were also in some degree contaminated by Anglicanism, liberalism and modernism. But those who were interested in Soloviev's ideas and made friends with Russian theologians who were keen students of the Greek Fathers and of Byzantine and Russian mystics, were not so certain that rules devised in the West since the Reformation applied to the conditions of the Russian emigration. They had the support of Mgr Andrew Szepticky, the Metropolitan of the Ukrainian Catholics in communion with Rome, and of other Eastern Catholic authorities among the Syrian Melkites, who wanted to make it easier for Orthodox to come into communion with Rome without repudiating anything in their own tradition. They accepted Soloviev's view of the schism as within the church, maintaining for instance that the schism in the Patriarchate of Antioch in 1724 between candidates recognized at Rome and at Constantinople was analogous to schisms between popes and anti-popes in the Middle Ages.[11] It ought not to have been consolidated into a permanent separation, and it could be healed without compelling the Orthodox involved to break completely with all their brethren who were not in communion with Rome.

The practical importance of these differences of opinion between Roman Catholics about the schism between East and West was reduced by the general belief that the Orthodox Church as an organization in Russia was near to extinction, and that in Syria, Palestine and Egypt, cut off from Russian support, it was slowly dying. In Greece and Romania, Serbia and Bulgaria it survived as a national institution, but the acids of secularization were bound to destroy it in time. The future of Christianity in Russia was most uncertain. It might take a long time to disappear. It would revive if the regime was overthrown, but this was unlikely to happen except after a military defeat that would throw the country open to Catholic and Protestant missions. Protestants had reason to believe that these would have some success, and Catholics that the Orthodox were ripe for conversion. Prayers for the conversion of Russia were regularly said after mass.

In the 1930s a German invasion of Russia seemed probable. In 1939 it was delayed, but in 1941 it actually happened. The welcome given to the German armies in many places confirmed the expectations of those who had long hoped for the collapse of the Soviet government. On the other hand the restoration of the Patriarchate of Moscow with Stalin's consent in 1943 opened up another possibility, and swiftly revealed the unexpected strength of Russian Orthodoxy.

No one has yet explained how the Russian church survived from 1923 to 1943. Most probably no satisfactory explanation will ever be given. A church that persists under pressures cannot keep records without grave danger to many of its members. There are like difficulties in reconstructing the history of the primitive church in the age of the martyrs.

11

Nearer our own time, the survival of the Roman Catholic Church in England and Wales is hard to explain, and explanations are conflicting. It is evident that towards the end of the eighteenth century Catholics themselves believed that their numbers were diminishing. Their recovery has been explained by the French emigration, by Irish labour, and by the Oxford Movement. An important factor was probably the effect of the industrial revolution on Catholic communities in Lancashire, south Staffordshire, and parts of Yorkshire, who took advantage of new opportunities to establish mass-centres with vigorous, vital and attractive congregations before the Irish arrived in large numbers, found a welcome in them, and provided priests for them. If records of this are scattered and difficult to find, reports of the persistence of Orthodoxy in the Soviet Union before 1941 are erratic and unreliable. They were not believed and they would be unbelievable if the church's strength had not become so evident after this. The problems concerning the relation of this to diocesan and patriarchal organization have never been made plain.

In the 1950s it was still easy to believe that the pre-condition for any kind of freedom in the Soviet Union was defeat in a Third World War. Those who had welcomed the Germans in 1941–2 and retreated with them in 1944 were bound to encourage this opinion. Many of them joined the 'Russian Church Abroad' and confirmed it in the hard line. On the other hand after the death of Stalin it became increasingly plain that the Orthodox Church was a problem to the Soviet government. An all-out attack would drive resistance underground, but Christians constantly had to be reminded of their powerlessness to withstand pressures, and of the dangers to priests who became centres of disaffection. Yet it also suited the convenience of the Soviet government to allow the Russian church to be represented in the World Council of Churches in 1961 and by observers at the Second Vatican Council in 1962–4.

In 1948 when the World Council was formally constituted

12

the Moscow Patriarchate condemned it as politically peril-
ous, an instrument of American policy, intelligibly as John
Foster Dulles was present, and took up a negative attitude
on the question of Anglican orders, which some Orthodox
churches had recognized as valid in the years between the
wars.[12] Many Roman Catholics, as well as Anglicans and
Protestants, regarded these decisions as determined by political pressures. Catholics were especially distressed by the
liquidation of Eastern churches in communion with Rome in
Romania and the Ukraine, and compared their compulsory
reintegration into the Orthodox Church with similar
measures taken by the Russian imperial government after the
partition of Poland in the eighteenth century. They might
have been wiser to pay attention to an even more exact
parallel in the situation of Christians in Muslim lands in and
just after the time of the Crusades. It was prudent then to
disown links with Rome, where the Pope appeared as the
Caliph, the political and spiritual head, of Western Christendom. Patriarchs of Antioch and Jerusalem repudiated plans
for the reunion of East and West at Lyons in 1274 and at
Florence in 1438–9, and yet did their best to remain on
friendly terms with Latin pilgrims, with the Franciscans who
came to Jerusalem in the fourteenth century, and with missionaries afterwards. They used the services of the Jesuits in
pastoral care and in the education of the clergy. This came
to an end only as the decline of Turkey led to contentions
between Russia and France for influence and to fears among
the Greeks of Constantinople that they would be the first to
suffer from any unrest and disorder among Christians of
their obedience. So the Orthodox in Russia make use of the
superior education of Ukrainian Catholics who stay behind
with them. To Ukrainians in exile it is a betrayal to stay in
Russia and communicate with schismatics, but another view
of the matter may be taken at the Russian college in Rome
where educational services are given to some Orthodox from
Russia.

Resentment against the incorporation of Eastern Catholics

13

in Orthodox churches not only in the Ukraine but in Romania remains an objection to the *Ostpolitik* of the last three Popes, who have all sought to detach the Holy See from political opposition to Communist governments. This has now been inherited by a fourth, who knows what life is like in a Communist country. It has to be seen in relation to hopes for a general reunion between the Orthodox and Rome, to the agreement between Pope Paul VI and the Patriarch Athenagoras for the lifting of the anathemas laid down in 1054 by Rome against the errors of the Greeks and by Constantinople against the errors of the Latins. The development of dialogue betwen Rome and the East has so far been impeded by the difficulties of communication between the Orthodox in Russia, and between Russia and Romania and the Orthodox elsewhere, in Greece, in Syria and the Lebanon, and in the Russian emigration, but these will not last for ever. We may then discover that the Orthodox objections to the papal claims are not to the Roman primacy itself or the infallibility of the church, but to the absence of sufficiently clear distinctions between the universal church, the Western Patriarchate, and Rome's original metropolitan province, that Rome has come to treat the whole West, and then the whole church, as subject to her own ordinary authority, and so to regard theological statements made in a particular and provincial context as though they were addressed to the universal church. Objections of this kind are more readily entertained in the new situation since the Second Vatican Council, where Orthodox influence was important, much more important than Anglican or Protestant, not only in regard to liturgical reform, but in the doctrine of the church and in theological method. In this last regard Russian objections to the use of scholastic methods borrowed from the West in the formulation of Orthodox arguments against Rome have contributed to the renewed study of the Fathers and of Byzantine and Western mystics not only in the Russian emigration but among French and German Roman Catholics. All this has helped to create an atmosphere in which the infallibility of the church and the role of the Pope in this can be seen in a new light, as having more to do with universal meanings and less with irreformable formulations.[13] There is little if anything in Roman Catholic doctrine that the Orthodox would wish to condemn, if it could be explained to their satisfaction, and less that is taught in the East and condemned by the West, but there is much that needs understanding.

We can no longer afford to leave out of our history either the Byzantine empire or the old Russia which is as important as Marxism for the understanding of the Soviet Union. With or without Communism this will remain different from the rest of Europe, and sensitive to the risks of penetration from the West, like the Byzantine empire and Muslim lands in the days of the Crusades. Other parts of the world have suffered from the delusions of Western colonialists that all that they bring is good for everyone. The papal primacy has suffered in reputation by association with Roman imperialism, not only in the medieval but in the modern Christian East, and in Latin America and Africa.

Imperialism has also influenced the self-understanding of the Roman church, but this in the beginning had little or nothing to do with the government. The Roman church was an illegal organization, operating mainly among aliens in the poorer quarters of the city, for more than two and a half centuries until 311. In the middle of the fourth century the Roman liturgy was still in Greek and it has never lost such Greek and Hebrew words as *Kyrie eleison*, alleluia and amen. By the end of the second century it was already customary for the bishops of churches in central and southern Italy, of Sicily and of other Italian islands to be confirmed and consecrated in Rome. The boundaries of this metropolitan province of the Roman church do not correspond with those of any administrative area of the empire, but most of the cities in it had been incorporated in Rome before the fall of the Roman republic. Their citizens continued to think of themselves as Romans after Rome ceased to be the centre of

15

government. Rome and the 'suburbican' churches were on lines of communication whereby cultures and religions had passed from East to West before the rise of Rome, through Etruria and the Greek cities of Italy and Sicily. These lines remained open after the fall of the Western Roman empire. Rome remained a centre of culture after political power had passed to Milan, Ravenna and Padua and to the new imperial city at Constantinople. Its political importance later was due to the Pope's regular contacts with the churches of his metropolitan province, whose bishops were important in the affairs of their cities, as he was and is in Rome.

No doubt Roman ideas of church government have been shaped by Roman law and the memories of empire, as well as by problems of administration in a large metropolitan area. But in Rome it is impossible to ignore the presence of other churches from other cultures. Greek monasteries continued to flourish and to be founded in and around Rome until the eleventh century.[14] Later in the Catholic Reformation there came to be Greek, Syrian, Russian and Ethiopian Colleges, while English and Irish Colleges continued to maintain the several identities of distinct Catholic communities.

It is possible to insist on these to the point of separation, not only in the East. English and Welsh Catholic exiles have contended for the control of the English College, and the Irish for their national existence as well as for their church and for the claims of a Catholic king. Rome has also impressed her own identity on strangers and pilgrims, not so much by police measures as by the fascination of the tombs of the apostles, the catacombs and the Colosseum. These speak in terms of universal meaning, and in this sense Rome is a spokesman of the past to the present outside her own communion and beyond Christendom. We can say 'Here is tradition'.

This book is based on lectures given in Rome in December 1977 under the auspices of the Centre for Indian and interreligious studies founded there in connection with Dharmaram College, Bangalore. The lectures were at the Pontifical Oriental Institute in the Piazza St Maria Maggiore, close to the Russian College, and most of those who heard them were Eastern Catholics in communion with Rome. It was therefore unnecessary to insist on the importance of Eastern Orthodoxy, and much of the material in this introduction was therefore reserved for an appendix on 'Rome and the Christian East' in the first edition of this book published at Bangalore in 1978. Of this I have kept the part about scholasticism. I am grateful to the Carmelites of Mary Immaculate, who invited me to give these lectures in honour of the priestly jubilee of Father Placid Podipara, for permission to revise them, and especially to Father Mundadan for his introduction to the original edition. It seems to me that the circumstances of their delivery and publication throw light on the role of the Roman church in the narrower and wider sense in ecumenical relationships. I do not think that my views on the nature and history of the schism between East and West have changed substantially since the first edition of my *Byzantine Patriarchate* was published in 1947. I was an Anglican then and still an Anglican when I revised it for the second edition of 1962. But as a Roman Catholic I have been able to say the same again, and in Rome.

☆ 2 ☆

Merchants, Monks and Missionaries

Merchants have played a large part in the diffusion of civilization, not only be taking goods and tools from cities into
camps and villages, but by introducing fresh skills and new
ideas, including religious ideas and practices that excite curi-
osity, enquiry and imitation. Indian Christians have reason
to be aware of this because of the close connection between
the earliest Indian Christian communities and Syrian merchants trading between the Near and the Far East, between
the Red Sea and the Persian Gulf on one side and Malabar,
Ceylon and Mylapore on the other, and also because of the
role of commerce in all modern relationships between India
and the West since the Portuguese arrived, with the Dutch
and then the English at their heels.

But for two reasons the influence of trade has not had a
very prominent place in the general history of the world and
of the church. Firstly, merchants are not heroes of saga. The
Vikings are remembered as pirates, not as traders, even by
their own descendants, although much of their plundering
was done to obtain trade goods that could be sold at a better
profit than the scanty produce of their own lands, amber and
walrus ivory. They wanted more from the Mediterranean
than unworked ivory would buy, and so they stole finished
goods on the way, Irish carving and English embroidery.
Abraham and Jacob behave like wandering Aramaean merchants. In Deuteronomy 26.5 the story is summarized: 'A
wandering Aramaean was my father; and he went down into
Egypt and sojourned there, few in number; and there he

18

became a nation.' Aramaeans who wander have generally something to sell. They have ready 'money of the merchant' to buy a sepulchre for Sarah in the cave of Machpelah (Gen. 23.6), and to buy corn in Egypt, where there was generally a surplus, even in years of famine elsewhere. In traditions preserved by Sextus Julius Africanus, who collected a great deal of information outside the Bible about such things as the succession of Egyptian dynasties, Abraham went down into Egypt for this before Jacob, who sent his sons twice to do it before he went down himself (Gen. 12.10–20, 41, 43, 46).[1] In Hebrew saga both are transformed into sheikhs with cattle and camels, a more respectable and warlike line of ancestors for a ruling class in Jerusalem and Samaria. That did not prevent later Mesopotamian merchants from identifying themselves with them, as they set out to seek a country, on earth or in heaven, by divine command: 'Get out of your country and from your kindred, to a land that I will show you,' in India or China or Turkestan, or at the end of the day in the kingdom of heaven. So Patrikios, who became Mar Aba, the Catholicos of Seleucia, 'came from the country of the Chaldees to perform the mission of Abraham,' according to Cosmas Indicopleustes, the ancient mariner who wrote his *Christian Topography* at Alexandria in the sixth century AD.[2]

Another reason for concealing the activity of merchants is that they have trade secrets. There is evidence that the supply of fish for the British market rose steeply before 1497, when John and Sebastian Cabot publicly announced the discovery of Labrador and Newfoundland, in order to rally British fishermen behind them against expected competition from France and Spain. As soon as the discoveries of Columbus in the West Indies and on the American mainland were known, further exploration of the coastline was certain, and explorers were bound to come where the Cabots had been fishing. What had been a trade secret could only be defended by widespread public support.[3]

A similar problem surrounds the date of Hippalus and the

19

discovery of the monsoon as a way of getting to India from Arabia and the Red Sea without hugging the dangerous coastline of Persia and Baluchistan. There is a story in Pliny's *Natural History*[4] of a freedman of Annius Plocamus, who was farming the taxes by the Red Sea in the reign of Claudius, that he was blown by a gale to Ceylon from the Persian Gulf in a fortnight. It has therefore been argued that the use of the monsoon was not known in the reign of Claudius (AD 41–50). But apart from the question of the date of this incident, which Pliny may have misplaced,[5] it does not follow that the monsoon was not known to experienced sailors because someone in the employ of the customs discovered it only be accident. According to another passage in Pliny, the route across the Indian Ocean was discovered in three stages, one associated with Hippalus who found the way from Ras Fartak in Arabia to the mouth of the Indus, another that went to Sigerus, south of Bombay, and a third direct to South India and Ceylon.[6] It seems on the whole most probable that the first and second routes were already known in the reign of Augustus, when from the Egyptian port of Myos Hormos 120 ships left for the East each year. The Roman coins found in India include a large number struck in his reign, but very few before. The Arretine pottery which has been found south of Pondicherry went out of manufacture about AD 45, and probably came there earlier in the century.

The older route to India was by way of Mesopotamia and Persian Gulf. A quantity of Indian pepper was already reaching the Mediterranean in the earlier half of the first century BC, and the demand for it had increased sharply by Pliny's time, not only as a condiment, but as a way of preserving meat.[8] The Alexandrian Sea route was a way of developing commerce with India and the Far East that cut out dependence on the Mesopotamian merchants who were subjects of the Parthian Empire. This Mesopotamian or Babylonian trade with India had developed earlier, before the time of Alexander the Great. Perhaps the earliest evidence of its extent from India itself is in the use of Aramaic in Asoka's inscriptions, which proves that it was already a familiar language in India in the third century BC.[9] When we come to the first evidence from Chinese sources of commerce with the West at the end of the second century and at the beginning of the first, in 128 and 91 BC, it is clear that much, if not all of the Chinese silk was sent by sea from the Persian Gulf to the Nabataean Arabs at their ports on the Red Sea, and so to Petra and through to Palestine and Syria.[10] The direct passage of goods from Mesopotamia to Antioch was much more difficult. When the Romans came to control Syria they often seem to have bought all goods brought to the frontier from Parthia and sold them again to their own Syrians. They were clearly not anxious to encourage contacts between Syrian merchants on either side of the frontier.[11] On the other hand they showed some anxiety to establish direct contact with India and China, not only by the sea route to India, but overland from the ports on the Black Sea to Turkestan and so to trading stations in Bactria, where Chinese, Indian and Mesopotamian merchants were found together and valuable trade goods could be exchanged.[12]

The Parthian subjects engaged in this commerce were certainly Mesopotamians, who in the time of the Parthian Empire were encouraged to penetrate to the tribes of Turkestan, allies and auxiliaries of Parthian power in Persia, who needed some of the arts and crafts of a superior civilization. It is not easy to say exactly what India and China needed from the West. The quantity of coin found in Indian sites, which seems to have been used not as currency but as bullion, rather suggests that other trade goods were not so acceptable. Coins could be made into necklaces and other ornaments in return for the spices and silks that were wanted in the West. But Western skills were also in demand, and some of the exports may have been slaves, girls for the courts of Indian kings, and craftsmen who could give instruction in building and carving. In the north towards Turkestan the need of trade goods is much more obvious, and trade with India and China as well as with the Roman and Parthian

Empires may well have been chiefly in raw materials which the tribesmen could not use, in skins and furs and metals. The Babylonians had ancient skills, not only in manufactures, but in the calculation of times and seasons, in the making of a calendar essential for any development of agriculture and gardening in northern climes where the seasons are delayed and much less certain than they are by the Mediterranean or the two great rivers, the Tigris and the Euphrates.

We know less about Mesopotamian merchants in general than we do about their Phoenician kinsmen whose activities are documented by Greek and Roman historians as well as in the Bible. But we know that they diffused an alphabet and the art of writing, the use of coinage of the kind that developed in the Mediterranean, and sciences connected with the calendar, with astronomy and astrology. They found these in India already. Chinese astrology is clearly independent of Mesopotamian, but there may have been exchanges between them.[13]

Jews were certainly involved in Phoenician trade. The evidence for this, apart from the biblical account of Hiram's dealings with Solomon, (I Kings 9.25–8), is as old as Herodotus in the first part of the fifty century BC, and it may be older if the Paraita inscription is genuine, with a date corresponding to 534–31 BC.[14] But the centre of the Jewish dispersion was in Babylon, where the Babylonian Talmud came to be written, and it is reasonable to regard the aptitude of the Jews for commerce, already well known and recognized in the first centuries BC and AD, as developed in Babylonia. The image of Babylon as a commercial centre, dramatically developed in the Apocalypse of St John, is commonly connected in Christian tradition with Rome. But I am not sure that a Jewish seer of the first century BC, who in all probability had never been to Rome himself, would see it in that way. Babylon was by then a very ancient centre of trade, and the list of trade goods in chapter 18 could be Babylonian: 'Gold, silver, jewels and pearls, fine linen, purple, silk and scarlet, all kinds of scented wood, all articles of ivory, all articles of costly wood, bronze, iron and marble, cinnamon, spice, incense, myrrh, frankincense' (Rev. 18. 12, 13). These are followed by the more ordinary articles of consumption, 'fine flour and wheat, cattle and sheep, horses and chariots, and slaves, that is, human souls'. These were less portable, and for their size less valuable, but silk is there, and the spices from India.

We may fairly assume that Jews were engaged in this trade already in large numbers. They had reasons for preferring commerce to other ways of rising in the world. Their religion made it difficult, if not impossible, to rise as landowners and members of city aristocracies, either in the Roman Empire or in Mesopotamia, except in some places like Adiabene, where Jews had connections with the royal family.[15] On the other hand they were exiles anywhere. They carried their law with them, and they did not have to leave behind them temples, oracles or shrines. Their God was as near to them in Morocco as he was in India or on the road to China. Everywhere they might meet brethren, and fulfil their vocation. Everywhere they might meet and keep proselytes. Jewish influence in places like Yemen and Ethiopia[16] certainly dates from this time if it is not earlier.

The first Christians in Babylonia were proselytes or God-fearers already attached to Jewish communities, like those that St Paul found on the highway of trade across Asia Minor and again at Philippi in Thrace, where Lydia, the seller of purples, very expensive goods, had come from Thyatira on the other side of the sea of Marmora (Acts 16. 14–15, 40). We know less about Christians in Mesopotamia. Their history in the second and third centuries is very obscure, and it has been argued that most of them were Gnostics or Marcionites, and that all fully-initiated Catholic Christians, were dedicated celibates, Sons and Daughters of the Covenant. The dedication of these to wholetime service, without any human attachment, was part of their rite of baptism. This seems to have some foundation in a very close association between their baptismal forms and their forms of dedication

23

to a consecrated life, but some association between them is found wherever vows are taken in the context of the eucharistic liturgy on such baptismal feasts as Easter day.[17] I do not myself believe that there was any time when no one was baptized who intended to continue in the married state, but a contrary impression can easily arise through concentration on the acts of the martyrs, neglecting those who under persecution move from place to place, following the precept, 'If they persecute you in one city, flee to another' (Matt. 10.23). Those who flee have to take something for travelling expenses, something not wanted in one place that can be sold in another, such as spare skins that can be turned into tents.

The various forms of the story of St Thomas are known to most Indian Christians, who know that they cannot all be historically true, but as a foundation story for Indian Christianity it is no doubt true to the facts that Western craftsmen were employed in skilled jobs, that they dealt in pearls of great price and other valuables, and that they attracted the attention of princes, who gave them positions and privileges.[18] The Christians had this advantage over Jews and Chaldean pagans, that they could incorporate Indians into their own community without making them Jews. They ran the risk of persecution in that they would not involve themselves in other religions, but perhaps less in India and Ceylon than in other places. In India everyone was accustomed to sects such as Jains and Buddhists, who had their own rules of worship, and caste barriers in any case made participation in rituals exclusive. The Christians came to be regarded as a special class or caste, with a knowledge of the ways across the seas that was of advantage to those who grew pepper and spices for the Western market, or imported Chinese goods for re-export to the West.

Some of our most interesting information about monks, merchants and missionaries arises from the diplomatic efforts of the Byzantine emperors to promote communication with China in some way that might bypass Persia. Persia was the one great power on the Roman frontier with whom the Roman Empire had to deal on approximately equal terms. It would be a mistake to imagine that they were always at war, either in the period of Parthian rule that ended in 225 or in the days of the Sassanids, who reigned in Persia for four hundred years after 227. The peace with Persia made by the Emperor Jovian, who in 364 left the important town of Nisibis, a centre of Christian culture, on the Persian side of the border, was only occasionally and intermittently broken between then and 526. It might well be argued that this was an important factor in the preservation of the Eastern Roman Empire in the fifth century, when the Western Empire collapsed altogether. The problem of defence in the East was limited to the part of the Danube frontier that lay in the Eastern prefecture, and the frontiers of Egypt and Syria, that were fairly easy to defend against nomads from the wilderness so long as a number of forts could be adequately equipped and manned. But when Persian ambitions to conquer Syria revived in the century between 526 and 629, imperial defences were so seriously damaged, not only in Syria but in Mesopotamia, that the whole of the fertile crescent was exposed to the inroads of hungry nomads. There would have been an Arabian invasion without Islam, though the conquerors might have been assimilated as earlier invaders from the desert had been, by the attractions of a superior civilization, if they had not developed a morale and religion of their own to keep them distinct.

It was in the period of the Persian wars that the Emperor Justinian endeavoured to enlist allies on both sides of the Red Sea, in Yemen and Axoum, to revive and promote Alexandrian trade with India,[19] and also to encourage trade with China through tribes like the Ephthalites who had Christian connections. We are told by Procopius in his *Gothic War*[20] of certain monks who told Justinian that while it was impossible to transport silk worms or moths from China, eggs could be brought. By generous promises he persuaded them to do this. According to a fragment from

25

another historian, preserved by Photius,[21] they kept them warm in dung concealed in their staffs, and 'at the beginning of spring put out the eggs on the mulberry trees that formed their food, and the worms feeding upon these leaves developed into winged insects and performed their other operations. Afterwards when the Emperor Justinian showed the Turks the manner in which the worms were hatched, and the silk which they produced, he astonished them greatly. For at that time the Turks were in possession of the marts and ports frequented by the Seres (the Chinese) which had been formerly in the possession of the Persians. For when Ephthalanus, King of the Ephthalites, conquered Perozes and the Persians, the latter were deprived of these places. Later the Turks conquered the Ephthalites.'

The implication of this story is that the Turks did not know what silk really was, and how it was made. We may suppose that the Mesopotamian merchants did, and that the monks had gone to China with them, in their caravans. But monks are not so interested as merchants in preserving trade secrets. It seemed to them a good idea to take the eggs of silkworms to a Christian country where silk could be produced successfully. The Byzantine silk industry came to be an important source of wealth and revenue, carefully controlled. This does not apply only to the care of cocoons and the breeding of silkworms, but to mechanical methods used in treating the silk. The Byzantine silk industry concentrated on the production of expensive articles of court dress, ecclesiastical vestments, and wrappings for relics, many of which have been unearthed from monastic reliquaries in recent times. Later, in the declining days of Byzantium, Byzantine methods of silk manufacture were practised at Genoa; where they became models for the pioneers of the English industrial revolution, who gave them a different direction.[22]

The *Christian Topography* of Cosmas Indicopleustes also reflects the anxieties of the age of Justinian about silk, before Byzantine manufacture began. He wrote it in Alexandria, and he clearly understood from his own experience the sea route down the Red Sea to Arabia and East Africa, but his theological associations and preoccupations are those of the East Syrians in Mesopotamia. He describes himself as a disciple of Patrikios, who became their Catholicos in the middle of the sixth century, and he reports on bishops 'from Persia' in India and on the land and sea routes to China. Where silk was concerned he did not believe that the sea route could compete with the land. He reckoned a hundred and fifty day marches, at thirty miles a day, perhaps more, from China to Persia, through the country of the Huns, 'India', and Bactria, as far as from Seleucia in Syria, the port of Antioch, to Spain. 'The Indian philosophers, those who are called Brachmanes, say that if a cord was stretched from Tzinista (China) to the Roman Empire, across Persia, this would divide the world in two, and perhaps they are right.'[23] He thought it much more difficult to traverse the Persian Gulf, the Indian Sea, and the other Gulf, larger than the Persian one, that is reached by turning to the left on the other side of Ceylon on the way to China. Clearly he had not been there, and his informants when in this instance they spoke of Tzinista, may have been referring to some port in Malaysia or Siam where Chinese goods were found.

Monks are not concerned with commercial profits, as merchants are. Cosmas in retirement, in a monastic milieu, was prepared to give information in reply to the objections of those Alexandrians who were so foolish as to believe that the world was round, and to ignore the difference between gulfs like the Mediterranean, the Red Sea and the Persian Gulf, and the inaccessible ocean surrounding the world. He was a friend of ascetics, and had acquired from them a large body of oral teaching, supplemented in retirement by some reading in the Bible and commentaries, especially those of Theodore of Mopsuestia, who was old-fashioned, and in Egypt unpopular. He was not a monk, but he liked to have monks with him, like Patrikios and Thomas of Edessa. He could have been a presbyter or even a bishop if he had settled down in some other place than Alexandria. Despite the prestige of monasticism on both sides of the Roman-Persian frontier, which led in time to the choice of monks as bishops everywhere in the Christian East, some traders were certainly presbyters, and some bishops. In the West regulations made at the Councils of Elvira and Sardica, held in the first half of the fourth century, refer to the problems of bishops away on business, presumably on trading voyages.[24] St Gregory the Great at the end of the sixth century was troubled by the activities of a bishop who was more interested in his ships than in his clergy.[25] In the West the requirement of celibacy for bishops, priests and deacons was made at an early stage, but little was done to enforce it before the eleventh century. In the Eastern Roman Empire a new law of the Emperor Justinian required married priests to separate from their wives if they were promoted to the episcopate, but this did not become a law of the Byzantine church until 692–3. At the end of the fifth century married bishops were certainly allowed and even encouraged in the East Syrian community.[26] In Mesopotamia however monks were commonly preferred, and in the seventh century the choice of a married bishop for an important see was regarded as an anomaly.

The married bishop in the Persian Empire is generally explained as a concession to the standards of the court and of the official religion, and to Persian prejudices against monasticism. It may have as much to do with the needs of mission stations at stops on the caravan routes, where stores were maintained for customers who came in to supply their needs, and often became aware of their need of the Christian gospel. What was wanted on the spot, to look after the store and the customers, was not a monk who had no sense of the value of goods, but a merchant and his wife who would stay there all the time, while caravans came and went, and meet the spiritual and temporal needs of those who came to the store in search of something to maintain their civilized standards.

Christianity in nomad lands was faced with practical problems. In many places no crops were grown, and wheat and wine were simply not available for the eucharist. Sometimes the missions introduced agriculture. We hear of an Armenian missionary who instructed his converts in the tillage of corn and vegetables. We also hear of a saint who was so accustomed to eating bread made of rice that he suffered from indigestion on returning to city life because in these countries he was 'accustomed to eat bread of rice only'.[27] He doubtless used this for the eucharist, but wine was a greater difficulty. The pouring of water over raisins was preferred to the use of the local intoxicant. There were also problems over fasting and abstinence.

It is clear that Christianity in Central Asia grew up out of the dependence of nomad tribes for some of their needs upon caravan traders, who took from them furs and skins in exchange for useful tools and graceful ornaments of life. This caravan trade continued, despite changes in political conditions both in Persia and in China, where emperors sometimes favoured, sometimes resented and persecuted, any alien influence from India or the West. Those who welcomed Buddhists also welcomed Christians. They suffered at the same time, but the Buddhists survived better because their religion was more capable of taking colour from the local scene and melting into a new form of Taoism. Mesopotamian traders were generally welcomed and seldom feared, even in China, because they were not regarded as agents of the Persian Empire or of the Caliphate in Damascus or Baghdad. They had standards different from those of the official religion of Persia, rooted in an older Chaldean civilization, and in communication with Byzantium and with other Christians in the West, despite some theological and ecclesiastical differences, which Christians in China,[28] India and Central Asia did not go out of their way to emphasize.

Perils came to them when Mongol conquerors from Central Asia invaded Mesopotamia in the thirteenth century, and promoted them to high positions over the heads of the Arabian Muslim aristocracy. Their influence with the Mongols, generally exercised through Christian queens, led to overtures for some kind of alliance between them and Christian powers, the Armenians of Cilicca, and the Franks who still held the principality of Antioch after they had been driven from Jerusalem. Central Europe was terrified of the Mongols, who had conquered Russia and threatened Poland, Hungary and Germany. Papal diplomacy was exercised in the hope that their attention could be diverted to Egypt, the Persian Gulf and the Indian Ocean, where they might break the back of Islamic power to the south of them. The Islamic world was then in great political confusion, and had every reason to be terrified of them, but Islam not only survived but succeeded in involving Turks and Tartars on her side against those tribes who had long adhered in some kind of way to East Syrian Christianity.

Some Turks had been Muslims before, as some were Buddhists, but in the fourteenth century, with Timur the Lame behind them, the Muslim Turks went from victory to victory. The stores on the caravan routes were destroyed. The ancient centres of Mesopotamian culture, which had long suffered in the confusion of wars between Muslim emirs and between them and the Mongols, were pillaged and ruined. Canals could not be repaired. In Palestine and Egypt Christians suffered a persecution unparalleled in the earlier history of Islam, partly as a reprisal for the Crusades, as we shall see, but also because of suspicions that they had favoured the nameless terror from the north whose power to penetrate south has always been overestimated in the fertile crescent, where Russians, like Franks, generally make mistakes.

From Alexandria into Egypt

Alexandria was a great centre of commerce and Greek learning, but not a Greek *polis*, a city in the proper sense, with magistrates and a territory of its own before AD 199, and then the municipal council operated only within the walls.[1] It was not a *polis* but a *politeuma*, a social centre for a large class of officials involved in the very complex administration of Egypt, and for an even larger class of business people who met the needs of this administration in various ways. They belonged to *gymnasia*, institutions of Greek education, that were also found in the provincial capitals of Egyptian *nomes*. The education given in these had a different emphasis from that found in similar *gymnasia* in Greek cities where a measure of autonomy survived, and public business was intelligently discussed. Alexandrian education was intended to sustain the identity of a class who thought of themselves as Greek, not Egyptian, but worked to maintain what was substantially the same Egyptian system of Government as had endured for centuries under the Pharaohs.

The story of Joseph throws light on this as the Hebrews saw it (Gen. 47.13–26). All Egypt belonged to the king or to the priests. The king gave seed corn to his tenants, and they had to give him part of their crops. All the beasts, cattle, sheep, horses, asses, were also his, because they had been in debt to him in the years of famine, and had been sustained by stores collected in the pyramids in the years of plenty. This interpretation of the situation is coloured by what happened in other places where poor peasants got into debt to the ruling classes, in Palestine as in Greece, and so became serfs. But in Egypt the power of the rulers over the cultivators of the soil had roots in the very nature of the soil itself. This was brought down every year by the Nile flood from Central Africa and distributed over the fields. The size of the inundation was known to the central government before it reached the cultivated areas, and the canals and dams, always kept in repair, were allowed to operate according to the measure of this particular inundation in this summer. Any attempt to interfere with the system to the advantage of any particular province or part of the royal estate could only lead to chaos everywhere else. This had happened in early times and had led to the fall of dynasties and to times of troubles, but then the system had to be made to work again.

The beginnings of this are difficult to date. Various dates are given for the establishment of a united kingdom by the first dynasty and the building of the pyramids by the third and fourth dynasties, but on any calculation more like three thousand than two thousand years intervene between these and the Persian conquest in 525–3 BC.[2] Under the Persians the Egyptian social structure remained substantially intact. The Ptolemies, who came after Alexander the Great's conquest of Persia, from 312 to 31 BC, tried to civilize their civil servants on Hellenistic lines, but they themselves as time went on became more like Pharaohs, they even married their sisters, at any rate officially and ritually, and bequeathed the throne to the queen's baby, whoever the actual father may have been. The king of Egypt must be born to an Egyptian queen and grow up under the protection of all the Egyptian kings and queens, lords and ladies of the soil, divine and human. Like Horus, the child god born each year to Isis, the widow of his dismembered father, Osiris, whose body was everywhere dissolved in the mud of the Nile, he owed his strength and vitality to his identity with the dead kings whose tombs stood and still stand on either side of the stream.

The Ptolemies, like other Pharaohs before them, spent some of the wealth of Egypt on adventure elsewhere. They had political and military ambitions in Palestine and Cyprus, Crete and Arabia, but much of their expenditure must have been within the country, and all rebounded to Egypt's glory. But the Roman emperors were non-resident landlords, who used their Egyptian possessions to reward their followers with profitable posts, and to promote their personal power in other parts of the Roman empire. As a result of this the cultural gulf between the higher echelons of the Egyptian administration and the tillers of the soil increased instead of diminishing. It is true that the Egyptian services became one of the models for the development of imperial administration in other provinces. It could be said that the Roman Empire was slowly Egyptianized, but it must have been much more obvious to the Egyptians that every year a larger part of their harvest went overseas to keep the Roman people happy, and to sustain the expenses of imperial administration.

These became heavier as time went on. The reasons for this have to do with the general history of the Empire, and especially with the increasing inability of municipal councils to meet their responsibilities in their cities and the villages dependent on them. All real responsibility for critical decisions fell into the hands of the provincial governors and their staffs, but the *curiales*, the councils of the cities, were still responsible for collecting revenues. If they could not do it, they themselves were made to bear the burdens of the deficit, except in Egypt, where the class who elsewhere were councillors were servants of the state. At the end of the second century AD they were made into *curiales*. Their *politeumata* and *gymnasia* were transformed into cities with town councils, so that they might bear the same burdens, but they were not given any new initiative or independence.[3] They had simply to choose from among themselves the *Decaproti* who in each *nome* or district saw to the repair of dams and canals, dealt with recalcitrant tenants, and saw to the dispatch of corn for shipment to Rome, while other magistrates chosen from the same class distributed seed corn, and superintended flooding and sowing. They themselves were imperial tenants

33

(sometimes nominally owners) of larger estates from which they had to make a living and maintain their position, but their responsibilities were becoming more and more burdensome. If they did their best to evade them, so did the poorer tenants, the fellahin. Both stood in dread of the *strategos*, the general in every *nome*, who was an imperial military officer, with special troops, the *frumentarii* or corn-corps, who acted something like the police in a modern totalitarian state.

The result of this was to break down the division between the Hellenized upper classes and the Egyptian poor. To a large extent they were both ground between the same millstones, and both driven to sympathize with subversion. In the third century AD one increasingly important subversive force was the Christian church. According to Alexandrian tradition this began in the poor part of the Jewish quarter of Alexandria. The first bishop, the original patriarch of Alexandria, was a cobbler called Hanania, who ran his needle into his finger while mending St Mark's shoes, and swore. The saint said: ' "If you will believe in Jesus Christ, the Son of God, your finger will be healed", and taking his finger said "In the name of Jesus Christ your finger is healed." At the same moment it was restored, for the flow of blood stopped.' This foundation story is found in the *Annals* of Eutychius, a late source of tenth century,[4] but it depends on something much earlier, very likely on the *Chronicon* of Sextus Julius Africanus in the third century.[5]

The Eutychian foundation story ascribes to St Mark the foundation of twelve churches with twelve presbyters, who not only elected but ordained the bishop until the time of Alexander, who was patriarch at the time of the Council of Nicaea, from 312 to 328. No doubt this is a simplification, but I see no reason to deny that there were presbyters and bishops in Alexandria for a long time before there were any other bishops in Egypt who could lay hands on them. Demetrius (190–233) was apparently the first patriarch of

Alexandria to consecrate bishops for Egyptian provincial centres.

We know a good deal about Demetrius in connection with the expansion of the church in the educated class in Alexandria itself. Clement of Alexandria and Origen taught there in his time, and Origen was in trouble with him. It is clear that the Alexandrian church already contained some very diverse social elements, including some of Egyptian origin, and that there were possibilities of conflict between them. Our present concern is with the expansion of the church from the streets of the city into the Egyptian countryside, on a small scale at first, since in 233 there were no more than three other Egyptian bishops. In 249 when the Decian persecution began, a special search was made for the bishops of important sees. At Rome, Antioch and Jerusalem they were immediately martyred. At Carthage St Cyprian disguised himself as a slave in his own country estate. Dionysius of Alexandria says in a letter:[6] 'that self-same hour Sabinus sent a *frumentarius* to search me out.' He waited for arrest at his own house for four days, while the search went on everywhere else. This shows that he was expected to escape into the country, as he eventually did, but he was caught at sunset on the first evening and taken to Taposiris. One of the boys who were with him was absent from the house at the time of his arrest. He returned to find the place under guard. As he ran off distracted, wondering what to do, he found a countryman on his way to a wedding party. We are not told that the countryman was a Christian. He may have been, but the wedding guests were certainly not all Christians. They had been having a good time and were at the top of their form. According to Dionysius 'they all with a single impulse, as if at a preconceived signal, rose up, and came running with all speed, and bursting in upon us they gave a shout, and the soldiers that were guarding us straightway took to flight'. When Dionysius and his friends, 'lying as we were on pallets without bedding,' first saw them, they took them for robbers and offered them their clothes. They expected nothing short of murder, but the bishop found himself put on a donkey and carried to a place of safety. It is clear from the tone of his letter that he expected and received criticism for being involved with gangs of roughs, in permanent conflict with the *frumentarii*, but he escaped arrest, and in later persecutions in the years that followed, when he was taken to places in the countryside such as Colluthion, 'a district without any brethren or persons of good character, and exposed to annoyances of travellers and incursions of robbers,' he found that in practice it was much more easy to communicate with Alexandria than it had been at Cephro and other places in Libya a few months before. Not only was it nearer but there were probably regular communications between the criminal classes of both neighbourhoods, the back streets and the wilderness. Letters were taken for prisoners by those who could not read them, but could carry them to any place in the city. The practice of sending prisoners to places on the edge of the desert seems to have fostered sympathy between them and others who were in such trouble that they went into the Sahara to find an oasis. There came to be an affinity between hermits and brigands, Christians and criminals.

The life of St Antony belongs to this period.[7] The traditional date of his birth is 251, but that may be too early, for he seems to have been still alive after 345. His family were by descent Egyptian noblemen, 'owners of slaves'. They had 'three hundred fields, a great estate with abundant crops', but they were themselves Christians, and encouraged the growth of the church in their village. They sent their boy to the *gymnasium*, but he did not make much progress in reading or writing, 'because he could not bear the rough behaviour of the boys; his whole desire was to be a simple man, and a dweller in tents'. According to St Athanasius, who wrote his biography, his relations with his family, as well as with those villagers who went to the church, were harmonious and happy, but 'he knew nothing of his father or of what went on among his own people. He was of so silent a disposition, that he did not trouble his parents by asking them questions. He was extremely shy, and honest beyond measure.' He felt himself unqualified to be a social climber, or even to keep on the ladder by the methods used by those concerned to maintain their position. If his parents recognized this, as they probably did, he must have been a problem child, though a very nice one. They died when he was nineteen, leaving him with a small sister.

Six months later he got the idea. He was thinking already, 'what shall I do with all this property', when he heard the words of St Matthew's Gospel, 'Sell all, and give to the poor,' (19.21). He distributed the three hundred fields among the people of the village, and sold the household goods, out of which he kept something for his own and his sister's use. St Athanasius in telling the story does not go out of his way to say what his original readers knew very well indeed without being told, that in such a redistribution of land a large number of regulations must have been broken. Very soon Antony found it necessary to disappear from his home altogether. He left his sister with the village virgins,[8] and 'lived alone in a house by the side of the village, at a sufficient distance therefrom, so that he might be somewhat apart from the habitation of men'.

He was not the only one. There were others in a like situation. The stories that follow show that he was obliged to go further from the village into the tombs and the wilderness behind the tombs. There his friends from the village brought him supplies, and found him exhausted by struggles against the powers from the past who lived in the tombs. 'One had the appearance of a lion, and another the form of a wolf, and of a panther, of serpents, vipers, scorpions, the lion roaring, the bull ready to gore, the panther ready to spring, the snakes hissing.'[9] All this went on for a long time, in a number of places, some of them at a distance from inhabited country. In these he seems to have attracted an increasing number of visitors, not only the inhabitants of his own village, who persistently brought him supplies from what they doubtless still considered to be his estate, but others who wished to see whether life was possible in oases. There are references to his little hoe. He could not have survived without doing a certain amount of gardening. There are also references to the displacement of snakes by the smell of his presence, but many more to his increasing understanding of the operations of demonic powers, who indeed possess a great deal of intelligence in human and natural affairs and have foreknowledge of the inundation of the Nile, since they know the extent of the rainfall in India, which means Ethiopia. But they are not infallible. They make mistakes, they may be wrong, and they clearly belong to the world of creation. The wilderness can be invaded and conquered by Christian men. It does not so belong to the ancient gods and the dead that any attempt to violate its borders must be finally disastrous. Rather the disasters must first come, and be overcome through patience and perseverance.

This was the best of news for those who wished to escape from the increasingly heavy burdens of the social system, from heavy taxation and forced labour, and to make an exodus somewhere. In Egypt and North Africa[10] there came to be an element in the Christian church drawn into it by hostility to the police. In the last great persecution, beginning in 297 and lasting intermittently until 313, the identification of martyrs came to be a problem. Some were not recognized by the authorities of the church on the ground that their death was not the direct consequence of any confession of faith, but of other offences. The same problem arises from time to time in the Soviet Union, when people are arrested on charges not directly connected with Christian propaganda or the education of the young, but for offences that would be disregarded if they were not subversive characters from the Communist standpoint.

The Meletians in Egypt were 'the Church of the Martyrs' in schism with the main body of the church of Alexandria. Their strength was evidently in the countryside. They had no use for speculative intellectuals or university men. The Patri-

arch Alexander took steps to depose Arius, the presbyter of
the church of Baucalis, whose lively sermons were followed
by the singing of controversial hymns, a characteristic activity of university congregations. Action was taken against this
partly, though not entirely, in order to convince the Meletians that if church and empire were now at last on the way
to peace, the church was not selling out to the philosophy of
this world. When Arius gained support in Palestine and Syria,
the Meletians, with other Egyptians, rallied behind Alexander. At the Council of Nicaea in 325, where Arius and his
associates were condemned with the good will of the Christian Emperor Constantine, the Meletians were reconciled
with the church.[11] But they produced a list of clergy to be
considered for future vacancies, with twenty-nine bishops of
country churches. This inevitably led to trouble when Alexander died in 328. This was the first election at Alexandria
under new rules, approved at Nicaea, that reduced the power
of the Alexandrian presbyters, and increased that of the other
Egyptian bishops.[12] Many of these had been Meletians, and
their status was in doubt. In Alexandria itself the deacon
Athanasius was a strong popular candidate, but the Meletians thought their man should have been chosen, and
renewed the schism.

In the troubles that followed the obstinacy of St Athanasius
in refusing any concession to Arius and his friends was due
not only to his sense of the importance of the theological
issues involved, but to the certainty that the Meletians would
exploit any concessions to the Arians to pose as champions
of a hard-line Christian orthodoxy against decay and world-
liness in the church reconciled with the state. The Meletians
were a gang, a guerrilla resistance movement. Athanasius
countered them with another gang, which used some ques-
tionable methods. Constantine at first supported him against
criticism from circles connected with the government, but it
was inevitable that the misdeeds of his friends should be used
against him by his critics, who wanted Arius restored and
theological controversy laid on one side as a strife about

words, in the hope that a vaguer version of the Arian approach would be acceptable to many new converts from paganism who were climbing on the Christian bandwagon, but still thought in a pagan fashion of gods and demi-gods. The story of the Mareotic Commission sent to collect evidence against Athanasius is not creditable to his critics, but he does not emerge unscathed.[13] In 335 he made his way to Constantine to appeal against the decision of the Council of Tyre that he should be deposed, with others who had been resisting the restoration of Arians. He caught the Emperor out driving, was summoned to sit with him in his chariot, and would probably have succeeded, as on previous occasions, in enlisting his support by his fundamental integrity and obvious insight, if his adversaries had not come armed with a report, probably new and certainly true, of a strike in the Alexandrian docks. At this point St Athanasius made a mistake. When the Emperor asked him if he had anything to do with it, he insisted that his concerns were purely religious, and denied that in the nature of the case he could have any influence over the dockers.[14] Constantine knew that this was nonsense, and sent him into exile at Treves.

But this took all the wind from the Meletian sails. Up to this point they could represent St Athanasius as the government's bishop. In exile he was not, and Athanasians and Meletians combined to make life impossible for any other bishops until Athanasius was allowed to return. When the Syrian bishops insisted that he had been lawfully deposed at proper councils at Caesarea and Tyre, he left for Rome in 341, maintaining that the patriarch of Alexandria could only be judged by the one other bishop of comparable or superior importance. The parallel between Alexandria in Egypt and the like position of Rome in regard to Central and Southern Italy and the islands round them had been explicitly recognized at the Council of Nicaea, where the rights of Rome and Alexandria were reserved in making provision for regular provincial councils elsewhere.[15] Moreover Rome was under a different emperor. This made it even more difficult to introduce another bishop into Alexandria, where the back streets were ready to demonstrate against any intruder, and agitators pursued by the police could always escape into the desert. By 346 Athanasius was back, still not recognized by Syrian bishops generally, but clearly supported by Rome and the West and by some lively 'little churches' in Syrian cities.

To rule Egypt with Athanasius in exile had twice been proved impossible, but it was now even more difficult to maintain the Egyptian social structure in its most important aspect for the imperial government, a large and regular supply of Egyptian corn, in face of the growth of Pachomian monasticism at Tabennisi from 323 to 346, and of other monastic centres where hermits and monks succeeded in maintaining themselves by an organized industrial life[16] in places where crops would not otherwise be grown, and taxation could not easily be collected. Some of these were Meletian foundations,[17] planned for resistance to government. Others who were non-co-operative while St Athanasius was in exile, were ready to help him and his friends at Rome, but not enthusiastically loyal to the Emperor Constantius II, who had Arian friends.

The case against Athanasius was that he had himself been involved in criminal activities during his gang warfare with the Meletians in 328–34. For these activities he had been deposed. He was not accused of heresy, as some of his friends were who had gone to the other extreme in resistance to Arianism. He was accused of crime, but he maintained that his primary crime was his opposition to those who wanted Arius back in Alexandria, his refusal to make any compromise with the friends and favourers of Arius in important sees in Syria and elsewhere. Because the Syrian churches maintained that he had been lawfully deposed, he did communicate with 'little churches' there who had gone to extremes as at Antioch, where the Eustathians led by the presbyter Paulinus gave him communion in 345 on his way back to Egypt.[18] But no one called him a modalist or an

41

adoptionist or a follower of Paul of Samosata. He was simply an impossible person to have as patriarch of Alexandria.

But his Egyptian friends would have nobody else. Even when they were confronted with a consensus of councils against him, not only in Syria but at Arles and Milan (with recalcitrant minorities of his friends and admirers), it was impossible to arrest him. When the police came to the church of Theonas in Alexandria in February 356, he asked them to allow the congregation to disperse, and when they had gone, he had simply vanished. This proved part of the government's case, and may well have won over Liberius of Rome to condemn him in 357.[19] His close connection with the criminal classes was proved in practice. But others in Cappadocia and Antioch were won over to the Athanasian view that Arianism was a more serious danger than anything at the other extreme. St Athanasius was not an extremist. He was ready to join in any orthodox alliance without quibbling over particular words in the creed of the Council of Nicaea, but this made the Government shy of any formulary that he could sign. They had to keep up a front against Athanasius that could not be identified with either extreme. The great majority of those who subscribed to the various official 'creeds' put out at the end of the 350s agreed with St Athanasius in substance, if not in words. 'The world groaned to find itself Arian' in the words of St Jerome,[20] for the Arians were a small party, though there was substance in the objections of St Athanasius that all the official statements were subject to misuse by them and by many more whose approach to Christian doctrine was coloured by their ancestral paganism.

Yet to rule Egypt against Athanasius was increasingly difficult. When Julian, the last pagan emperor, gave the Alexandrians a free hand the pagans killed his rival, George of Cappadocia, who was universally unpopular. St Athanasius died in possession ten years later.

☆ **4** ☆

The Kingship of Christ in Egypt and Babylon

Alexandria is not Egypt. Not only the official classes, the professors and students at the Alexandrian schools, but the well-to-do businessmen, and most of the artisans and small tradesmen would have repudiated any idea that they were 'inhuman' Egyptians in the first and second Christian centuries, and probably in the first half of the third. Egyptian solidarity behind the church and the patriarch does not come into existence much before the fourth century, and reaches its height in the fifth and sixth.

Yet Alexandria is in Egypt, and cannot escape the peculiar impact of Egypt. In 1963 I went to a *Son et Lumière* programme where the Sphinx recited the poetry of Alexander Pope. On the next night she spoke classical Arabic. It was impossible to avoid the sense that we were all contemporary to the pyramid builders, the classical poets, and the audience. Egypt is timeless, because the desert is timeless and so are the temples and the tombs, most of them in perfect condition after centuries of tomb-robbing. Papyri keep on turning up with personal stories from every century, but they are all contemporary. To say that there is no sense of history in Egypt would be absurd, but history itself is timeless, a series of repetitions. All the kings are the same king of the dead who every year was and is dismembered and scattered in the fields. The life of the land was and is the inundation coming down from Ethiopia, giving birth to the living corn, to the new king, who is the old king over and over again.

Alexandrian Greek literature is coloured by this, a long

series of epic poems after the manner of Homer, but of Homer interpreted, with all other Greek mythology, in allegorical and mystical senses related to the progress of the soul through life in this world to freedom among the immortal gods, reborn again to repeat the cycle. The Bible lends itself to this timeless reading in this setting.[1] To the Jews who made it Abraham's visit to Egypt was a prophecy of Jacob and Joseph, of their own captivity and escape. Their own imprisonment there and escape therefrom was a prophecy of their exile and return from Babylon, and this itself became a foreshadowing of their own ultimate return to the promised land. But in Alexandria all these types and symbols of a promised future began to be read as signs of something eternal and timeless, of the coming of the elect soul from the heavenly places to journey through the pains and tribulations of this present world, and so find her way back to her true home in heaven. Bodily life is a tomb in which penal duties have to be performed. We are all obliged to fulfil our daily tasks, to make bricks, generally without straw, but we shall in the end be delivered from the body of this death.[2]

Egyptian Christians were for the most part critical of the sophisticated allegorical interpretations of Origen and others in the Alexandrian schools, but they shared in the conviction that this life is a painful and laborious one, in the hope of deliverance through another Moses, a Messianic figure, cradled as he was in the bulrushes by the Nile, and nursed and tended there by the Mother of God who had wandered there as an exile after the massacre of the innocents in Bethlehem. The old gods of Egypt had fallen down before them.[3] This mother and child had become the hope of the oppressed, of the Egyptian underworld in city and country alike. The virgin birth of Christ was imagined and portrayed in terms that were inevitably coloured, not only by the birth of Horus to Isis who nursed him in secret, but by other stories of kings who were gods from birth.

The theology of Egyptian divine kingship is most clearly expressed in a series of paintings made under the direction of Queen Hatsheput, the sister and wife of Thotmes II, who maintained her power for some years after his death.[4] She sought to make explicit the legitimacy of her rule by showing that her father and mother had performed all the proper rituals involved in the propagation of a crown prince before she was born. As a princess she had been nourished with the milk of all the right sacred cows. She was the child, not simply of the royal family, but of all the gods. No doubt her claims were disputed, and the pictorial proofs for them elaborately concealed, but their controversial character underlines the essential idea that the Egyptian king was divine from birth to death. Indeed he was so sacred that his personal abilities did not matter. Pepi II came to the throne as a small boy. We have texts showing his keen interest in the preservation alive of a captured pygmy he wished to see.[5] He died in extreme old age, but the administration of his kingdom continued to function while he was senile, as it had during his childhood. There was no problem of the effect of the king's infirmities on his royal function. This was more likely to arise when Egyptian kingship was imitated in other and lesser monarchies, where the king had not the advantage of a large and loyal administrative service, although no doubt the displacement of dynasties might be the result of the king's mistakes in falling foul of his powerful ministers.

The Egyptian Pharaoh was more than a god. He was in his reign the living human incarnation of all the gods. After 523 he was no more, but his mythical memory was more powerful than ever. No doubt he was identified with Alexander the Great, who believed that Amon-Ra had recognized him as his son,[6] but none of the successors of Alexander could fill the bill. The Ptolemies were too Greek to be real Pharaohs, and Augustus Caesar was an alien in Egypt. But in his time a small boy played by the Nile who was indeed divine. That some simple Egyptians had recognized him and worshipped him came to be a tradition fostered among a few humble people in Alexandrian back streets. Its potency took two hundred years to develop, but the very eccentricities and heresies of early Alexandrian Christianity bear witness to the power of the idea of a total concentration of godhead in a human body, born of a woman, the Mother of God, and born to die, dismembered but communicating his divinity to others who consume him in the form of corn and wine.

The influence of Egypt on philosophy and theology, pagan and Christian, was felt indirectly through Alexandrian developments in Platonism, which certainly gave a new turn to the role of the soul and of the heavenly world in the Greek philosophical outlook, but the influence of Egypt on the Christian religion was direct and indirect. The diffusion of the cult of Isis was an indirect influence. The temples of the Egyptian queen in the back streets of so many Hellenistic cities were only imitatively Egyptian, but the Christianity of the Egyptian countryside must have been deeply coloured by its background, not only in the imagination of angels and demons, but in the idea of God suffering and dying in human shape and communicating to us the fullness of his life, made man that we might share his divinity with him. The Christ of Alexandrian theology was a real human baby, who had been in Egypt with Mary, and a real sufferer on the cross of his torture, a crucifixion no doubt inflicted on many Egyptian martyrs, but his humanity and divinity were so close to each other that they were almost completely fused. If he had a human soul, this was a perfect and entire one, who had been dancing in heaven and had never been out of step when the Word of God took him and brought him down to earth. Other souls were obliged to endure the limitations of existence in a variety of spheres because they had stepped out of line, and needed to be restored by discipline.

This discipline was indeed differently conceived by those who saw the world itself as a consequence of some primordial calamity, and those who saw it as fundamentally good, a place of education. These were both Christian and pagan.[7] The difference between them, which was indeed fundamental, was between those who saw the soul's salvation as his or her own work, the reward of free choice and labour, and those who saw salvation as the gift of God in Christ. It seems most likely that both were influenced by the impact of Jews and Judaism on the Alexandrian scene.[8] What the Jews had done was to show that a monotheistic form of religious belief and practice was practically possible. This could be intellectually respectable, but this was in itself a source of despair rather than of hope, of a sense of the inaccessability of the utterly unseen. The Christian saw him in action coming towards us not only in terror but in tenderness, if they were Gnostics, to save us from this world, if they were orthodox, to redeem the world and restore all to its original perfection.

The Babylonian approach to the idea of a divine king was a different one. It seems to me that this has been misunderstood by modern historians, Protestant and Catholic alike, because of its appeal to a kind of modern Christian whose primary interest is in the life of Christ as an historical human being, in the gospels as biographies of him. The Mesopotamian Christians of our first lecture lived in close contact with Babylonian Jews, and also with the Chaldeans who maintained the traditions of ancient religions in the Mesopotamian cities, and especially of the cult and study of the stars, of astronomical cycles under zodiacal signs, of the succession of eclipses, and of all the observations necessary for a correct calculation of agricultural operations, and for making the horoscopes of individuals. Mesopotamian history was a story of empires rising and falling in succession. No doubt the stages of this were very imperfectly known, but some sense of linear progress from empire to empire was common, and for Babylonian Jews related to a narrative that included Noah and the flood, the kingdoms founded by Nimrod, the tower of Babel, and all the ancestors and relations of Abraham. In Babylonian Jewish traditions these narratives were expanded to include other materials, some of them from the traditions of other nations, including traditions of judges and hero-kings raised by divine power to reign in their lands. The idea of the Lord's anointed, sent to deliver his people from peril, was not altogether peculiar to Israel. No doubt the Israelites persisted in loyalty to their own God after their national independence was lost, but their hope for a new Moses, a new David, another Messiah, who could do for them what David and Solomon, Hezekiah and Josiah, Zerubbabel and Nehemiah, had done before, was not altogether out of harmony with the hopes of other nations who treasured historical memories and watched for signs of the times.[9]

To Christians with this kind of cultural background Jesus the Messiah was indeed much more than a man. He was born of a virgin, and anointed by the Spirit. His death and resurrection led to his ascension into heaven, where Christians who shared his baptism were risen with him. They saw his relation to Almighty God in terms of his anointing by the Word and Spirit at his baptism, and of his ascension to sit at the right hand of the Father. The virgin birth was important, but chiefly as a sign or prophecy of this. They were sure that Jesus was not a God disguised in a mantle of human flesh. They were especially antagonistic to those who would depreciate or deny the inheritance of the Old Testament, which was an important part of their own history in the fertile crescent of Mesopotamia and Syria.

Egyptian Christians were loyal to the Old Testament, but in a different kind of way. To them it was the Jewish and Christian holy book, superior to the Greek classics, to Greek philosophy and Egyptian mythology, both in theological truth and in antiquity. But they were not so much concerned with the succession of historical events. Indeed in the parts that concerned Egypt, the plagues did not make literal sense, and like the hardening of Pharaoh's heart, demanded spiritual interpretation. At Alexandria they were treated as analogous to episodes in Homer that were incredible and morally shocking.[10] They believed that the captivity and the exodus had happened, but that their real significance was as signs of the eternal realities, our captivity, our exodus. So the presence of God in human flesh to redeem his people was the heart of the gospel, rather than the historical fact that he had come in humility and would come again in glory.

The other approach is commonly called Antiochene as distinct from Alexandrian, but this name is unfortunate. Antioch was a church with a long and honourable history, documented at the very beginning in the Acts of the Apostles and the letters of St Ignatius; it always contained a complexity of elements, Jewish and Gentile, Syrian and Greek. In the hinterland of Antioch little village churches were soon established, very like synagogues in their practical arrangements.[11] Some of them no doubt were almost completely Jewish, but in sharp conflict with orthodox Jews.[12] They must have had some influence on developments in Antioch itself, but Antioch was a Greek city, in contact with other Greek cities on the coast line at Seleucia, in Cilicia and in Asia Minor, and an important centre of administration. In the church of Antioch the liturgical language was Greek, but there were problems of interpretation to elements in the congregation who knew only Syriac.[13]

The beginnings of conflict between Alexandrian and Syrian approaches go back to differences between Origen and Sextus Julius Africanus over the interpretation of scripture, and the place of the story of Susanna in the Old Testament.[14] Africanus, despite his name, belonged to Syria. He came from Nicopolis in Palestine and had friends at Edessa. He was a pioneer in constructing a chronology of biblical history to which other traditions contributed, as well as books by Berosus and Manetho on Babylonian and Egyptian history, and he was evidently critical of excesses in mystical and spiritual interpretation.

The conflict over christology at Antioch began with the choice of a bishop in or before 260. Paul of Samosata was a *ducenarius* in the civil service of the kingdom of Palmyra, which at this time had taken over Roman Syria and was building it up as a buffer state between Rome and Persia, dismantled by the Emperor Aurelian in 270–2. Paul as a *ducenarius* had an office where virgins of the church were employed as secretaries. Some inevitable confusion between this office und the headquarters of the church resulted, with criticism of the virgins by other virgins and by widows. This led to conflicts which took a theological turn when Paul objected to some of the modern hymns sung in Christ's honour, and when his supporters began to acclaim him at his entry into the church building.[15]

A conflict developed between him and some of the presbyters, led by Malchion, a man of considerable learning in Greek literature and theology, who was certainly acquainted with the writings of Origen, and enlisted the support of bishops elsewhere, especially in Palestine, where Origen had taught at the end of his life, and at Alexandria, where his pupils were now influential. The charges against Paul were pressed at a series of synods at Antioch itself, between 262 and 268, but he had support in the city and was not easily displaced while the Palmyrenes were in control of the government.[16] His supporters were still in possession of the church plant when the Palmyrenes were expelled, and Paul with them. Clearly his christology was based on an interpretation of the Old Testament in which the Word and Spirit were both regarded as attributes of God. The Word of God was in Christ from his conception (I see no reason to believe that Paul denied the virgin birth), but Paul laid a special emphasis on the baptism of Christ, regarded as the prototype of our own. The Word of God in him and in us was identical with God's own Word of Power, and of one being (*homoousios*) with God himself.[17] Christ was not to be regarded as a distinct *hypostasis*, a second God. Paul was condemned as an adoptionist, identified with Jewish Christians who regarded Christ as a human Messiah, adopted by God as his son, but no doubt he repudiated this ancient 'Ebionism', and denied that he had ever said that Christ was a mere man. However he saw the centre of Christ's personality as human. I see no reason to believe that he was influenced by Origen's speculations about Christ's pre-existent human soul.[18] His background was in a different tradition, championing the divine unity against Zoroastrian dualism and popular pagan polytheism.

The alleged connection between Paul of Samosata and Lucian, martyred at Antioch in 308, rests entirely on a letter from Alexander of Alexandria to Alexander of Byzantium, preserved by Theodoret.[19] This most probably refers to another Lucian, who was head of the 'little church' of Paul's disciples after his death. But this little church made its peace with the main body at the Council of Nicaea, like the Meletians of Egypt.[20] Both these groups of dissidents approved of steps that were taken against the Lucianists, the disciples of Lucian the martyr, and especially against Arius, who was one of them.

Conflict at Antioch between Lucianists and others developed before and after the Council of Nicaea. Eustathius, who was elected bishop there in 324 against Lucianist opposition from Eusebius of Caesarea and others, and deposed in 329 or 330 under Lucianist influences, was clearly critical of mystical interpretation of scripture at Alexandria and elsewhere, and probably critical of the means used for identifying holy places by Constantine's mother, the Empress Helena, since he was accused of insulting her.[21] At Nicaea he was allied with Alexander of Alexandria, Hosius of Cordova, and other bishops from East and West, against the Lucianists, a group of intellectuals, suspected of trying to make the Christian faith conform with the categories of Neo-Platonism, by turning the Word and the Spirit into demi-gods, gods in the old pagan sense of archangels in the heavenly host, all in harmony with the ground of being. But Eustathius and Alexander did this from different traditional approaches. Arius and Alexander were both Egyptians, both Alexandrians, in some ways very close to each other. That is why St Athanasius was so sensitive to the perils of Arianism. Arianism was his own temptation, the temptation to construct the image of a god accessible to us as we are, knowable and understandable, with whom we can be united without being changed. Eustathius and his friend Marcellus stood[22] for the opposite idea, that the Word of God was united with the Second Adam, with the Son of Man in our nature and flesh, and so with us. St Athanasius agreed with them that Christ is human and divine, and not a god. But he had little to say about his human person or human soul. This may be because he was wary of Origen's speculations on pre-existence. No one accused him of heresy, as they did Marcellus, his disciple Photinus, and the 'little church' at Antioch who were loyal to Eustathius. But he was compromised by association with them.

Rome was slow in seeing objections to Marcellus and Photinus as well as to St Athanasius, and very slow to disown the Eustathians.[23] Her role in the controversies of the fourth and fifth centuries was not to initiate, or immediately to discriminate, but to discover what in the long run could be consolidated as part of the tradition. Immediately she made mistakes, not only over Marcellus, but over Vitalis, who first made a schism over the ideas of Apollinaris. She sent him to Paulinus and the Eustathian group at Antioch, who were not good judges. But she reserved judgment over proposals for compromise, and so kept the way open for a return to the creed of Nicaea, even if the creed of Constantinople, which we all now call Nicene, is not in all respects the creed of the Council of Nicaea in 325. Rome was more obstinate about the authority of Nicaea than St Athanasius, for it is in the Roman tradition that what has been said with authority has been said. It may need to be said again in a rather different form, but it cannot be dropped or contradicted without bringing discredit on the authority concerned.

☆ 5 ☆

The Monophysite Question

In the Arian controversy there was much confusion over the meaning of words, but little difficulty in recognizing Arianism as a heresy when once it was stated in a form implying difference, not only distinction, between the divine status of the Father and of the Son. No doubt there were many who accepted and used the formularies accepted and endorsed at Rimini and Seleucia in 359, and enforced for the time being by the authority of the government, who were not Arians themselves and did not think them Arian. On the other hand it seems fair to say that those who continued to adhere to them after the triumph of Nicene orthodoxy in 381, not only among the German auxiliaries of the Roman Empire, but in other places in East and West, did so because they found the idea of gods familiar and in very much easier than the new and strange idea that the one ground of being, the ultimate God, was in fact in action in this world.

The controversies of the fifth century have a different kind of history. They are said to arise out of differences between Alexandrian and Antiochene approaches to the reading of scripture and to the person of Christ. I have suggested in the last lecture that for these terms we should substitute Egyptian and Mesopotamian approaches to world history and divine kingship. Both were rooted in traditions that included Gentile as well as Jewish elements. The Jewish element is perhaps more evident in Mesopotamia than in Egypt, but we must not underestimate the debt of Origen to Alexandrian Judaism and to the study of scripture with rabbis in Palestine,[1] or the element in Egyptian religion that was attracted to apocalyptic visions of the end of the world.[2]

The Nestorian and Monophysite controversies arise out of real tensions between orthodox traditions. Both sides believed with equal intensity that Christ was God and man. As a result of the struggle with Arianism both were equally certain that he had taken upon himself the whole of human experience, that he had been born as a baby and suffered on the cross, and that in human flesh, and not simply in an appearance of this, he was risen from the dead. But Nestorius saw an Apollinarian leaning in St Cyril's way of putting this,[3] and St Cyril saw a renewal of Paul of Samosata's heresy in the objections of Nestorius to the use of the word *theotokos* of the Blessed Virgin.

When the news of the controversy between them reached Rome, Pope Celestine was unwilling to trust reports from Marius Mercator, the agent of St Augustine in Constantinople, who was keeping an eye on exiles from Italy and Sicily.[4] These Pelagian adversaries of St Augustine and St Jerome had been staying with Theodore of Mopsuestia, who had provided them with much of their ammunition for controversy. They were now seen on the steps of the patriarchal palace of Constantinople, where Nestorius was writing to the Pope asking him what the Pelagian controversy was.[5] This itself may have prejudiced Celestine against him, but he was too prudent to believe all that Marius Mercator said. He consulted John Cassian, one of St Augustine's critics who came from Thrace and had been in the East. Cassian had lately encountered a form of adoptionism,[6] a heresy easily scented in these Egyptian and Syrian circles from which he derived his monastic ideals. He wrote Nestorius off as another adoptionist like Marcellus, Photinus and the Eustathians in Antioch, whose opposition to Arianism had led them to fuse the three persons of the Trinity into one person of God. Where Cassian agreed with St Cyril and the Augustinian Marius Mercator, Rome came down on the same side, but when the Syrians who came late to the Council of Ephesus insisted that St Cyril's anathemas against Nestorius were open to objection as implying that the Son of God himself was subject to suffering, as the Arian Christ had been, and that some distinction must be made between the Son of God and the Son of Man who was crucified and risen,[7] the church of Rome welcomed, and probably indeed promoted,[8] overtures for understanding between the Syrians and Egyptians who had taken opposite sides at Ephesus in 431. The Syrians agreed that Nestorius had erred, and that he could not possibly be restored to the see of Constantinople, while St Cyril accepted a formula drawn up by his friend Theodoret, in which two ways of looking at the union of God and man in Christ were regarded as legitimate. What was common ground was belief in a union of two natures, divine and human.[9]

In 430–33 communications between Rome and Alexandria were not easy. The Vandal conquest of Africa had already begun, and must have made them difficult by land and sea. But the two cities and churches were still in touch with one another, and hoped for an early resumption of regular shipping through the summer. In 446–7, when controversy at Constantinople was beginning between the Patriarch Flavian and the Archimandrite Eutyches, who accused him of repeating the errors of Nestorius, regular sailings had been interrupted by the Vandals for some years. The trouble came to be concentrated on the authority of the formula of peace accepted by St Cyril in his letter to John of Antioch in 433. To Flavian this was the last word on the subject. Eutyches objected to its use to shield expressions employed by the friends of Nestorius, and condemned, explicitly or by implication, at the Ecumenical Council of Ephesus in 431. The agreement of 433 was of less authority. St Cyril was a big enough man to make it. He had something of the same largeness of mind that enabled St Athanasius to agree with others who opposed the Arians, but not in the same terms. His successor Dioscorus, who became Patriarch of Alexandria in 444, had a narrower outlook. He made the initial mistake of sympathizing with Eutyches, a muddle-headed extremist whose views could not be defended.

Eutyches insisted that *ek ton physeon*, of two natures, accepted by St Cyril in 433, must mean 'two natures before the union, one afterwards'. Moreover he would not say that Christ as *homoousios* with ourselves, as well as with God the Father, though he hesitated to deny it outright.[10] Both Flavian and Eutyches wrote to Rome, where St Leo wrote his *Tome* in reply to both of them.[11] No doubt it is magnificently written and applied to their situation, a very clear-headed piece of theology. But St Leo did not see this situation in a wider context. He probably did not know much about the development of criticism of St Cyril by Theodoret and others since his death, and the sensitiveness of his disciples to this. Instead of interpreting and defending the agreement of 433 he insisted on 'in two natures, without change, without confusion, without separation, without division', eternally distinct. Dioscorus did not expect this, and at the Second Council of Ephesus in 449, which he had already rigged to prevent the kind of schism that had taken place between Syria and Egypt at the First Council, he simply suppressed the Pope's letter. According to Michael the Syrian, a Monophysite historian of the twelfth century, who used early sources, he did so because he did not want to quarrel with Rome. He assumed that St Leo had blundered, and that the traditional alliance between Rome and Alexandria could be repaired when he grasped the situation.[12] But St Leo insisted that to accept the *Tome* must be at any rate one touchstone of orthodoxy. He would have preferred to see it accepted as orthodox on all sides, without a further Council,[13] rather as the formulary of Theodoret, presented to St Cyril by John of Antioch, had been in 433. But the way in which this had been challenged by Eutyches showed that private understandings where not enough. An Ecumenical Council was necessary, of more weight than the Councils at Ephesus in 431 and 449. When it met at Chalcedon in 451, the government insisted[14] on a definition of doctrine that could be used to determine orthodoxy, and the representatives of Rome insisted that at the key point in this the language of the *Tome* should be used, 'in two natures', and not the language of Theodoret, accepted by St Cyril, 'of *(ek)* two natures'.[15]

The Monophysite controversy was generally interpreted in the West in terms of the *Tome*, as if Nestorius and Eutyches were the typical heretics on one side or the other. St Leo himself did not do this, and may have regretted the rigidity of his legates. In a letter to the Alexandrians in 458, a few years later, he explained his understanding of the incarnation in St Cyril's terms and avoided using 'in two natures'.[16] But by that time Dioscorus had died in exile, deposed after he had attempted to condemn Leo as a heretic at Nicaea, just before the Council of Chalcedon,[17] and his successor, Timothy Aelurus, had been installed by his supporters among scenes of violence. They treated Dioscorus and Timothy Aelurus as the rightful successors of St Athanasius, Theophilus, and St Cyril. Proterius, the Chalcedonian patriarch intruded in place of Dioscorus, was like those who had been intruded in place of St Athanasius. He was killed in a riot by a stray brick, and this made any compromise much more difficult. It was impossible for the government to recognize Timothy Aelurus, who was with the rioters, as the lawful patriarch of Alexandria. He naturally preferred to suffer for orthodoxy, which the Chalcedonians called heresy, than for riot and murder. But in his absence under arrest the administration of Egypt ground to a halt, as in the days of St Athanasius.

This was inconvenient for Constantinople, where overtures had to be made from time to time to meet the discontents of Egyptians and others who resented the terms of the Council of Chalcedon.[18] These were regarded at Rome as selling out to Eutychianism, as subversive like earlier concessions to Arianism, the more so because the Roman aristocracy as well as the Roman church resented the reluctance of Constantinople to spend Eastern resources in sheering up a decaying Western Empire. This led to the Acacian schism between

Constantinople and Rome from 484 to 518. In this Rome had sympathizers in the East, who shared the approach of the Mesopotamians and of some other Syrians to the problem of Christ's human nature, and therefore supported the position of Chalcedon, and approved of St Leo's *Tome*.[19] This was a more important, a more final document for the West after his death. St Leo was a big enough man to reword it in his second *Tome* to the Alexandrians in 458, as St Cyril was a big enough man to write to John of Antioch in 433, accepting Theodoret's formulary. But Popes after St Leo could not shift from the most important piece of dogmatic theology that the Roman church herself had produced.[20] There were some in the West however who thought the Roman approach to Eastern problems too rigid, and that St Cyril, never fully understood, was in danger of being neglected.[21]

The Emperor Justinian, who succeeded his uncle Justin in 527, had already helped to restore communion between Constantinople and Rome in the first years of Justin's reign. Justin and Justinian were from Illyricum, the Latin-speaking province on the eastern side of the Adriatic, and wanted to restore the Western Roman Empire. Justinian succeeded in conquering North Africa from the Vandals, but found the restoration of imperial administration in Rome and Italy a far more difficult task than he expected, since so many of the peasants resented the exactions of their landlords, increased by the demands of the imperial tax-collector, and preferred the presence of Ostrogoth soldiers, resisting Justinian's armies. These acted rather like brigands in modern times, making demands for protection against the rent-collector, but more modest demands than those of landlords with a higher standard of living, who were required to restore and maintain an administration which had broken down.

Justinian therefore had a great deal of opposition on his hands in many parts of his empire, and much of it came from those who were opposed to the language of the Council of Chalcedon, but not to the substance of the doctrine defined there. They were prepared to condemn Eutyches,

Apollinaris and Nestorius, and they generally wanted something said against Theodore of Mopsuestia and others who had encouraged Nestorian ideas, and against severe criticisms of St Cyril by Theodoret and Ibas of Edessa. But they did not generally insist on anathematizing the *Tome* of St Leo or the Council of Chalcedon. They rather insisted that 'in two natures' ought not to be insisted upon, that the language of 'one nature of the Word that was made flesh' or of 'one nature out of two, divine and human', was more acceptable.

In Egypt it was impossible to impose a Chalcedonian patriarch, and no attempt was made until 537, under pressure from Rome, where the moral support of the church was needed for the campaign against the Ostrogoths. But elsewhere, especially in parts of Syria, there was much resistance from those who shared Egyptian objections. The leaders were all monks, austere ascetics, who would only gain support if they were imprisoned or exiled. Justinian sought to meet them by another tactic altogether. His wife Theodora shared their views, but also her husband's passion to restore unity to the church. She kept a collection of Monophysite ascetics in one of her palaces, where no doubt they maintained their austerities, but lost some of their reputation with their followers. They were guests of an empress who had been in show business, and was still pursued by scandals from her past. They were also engaged in conversations with those supporters of the Council of Chalcedon who were ready to do something to meet their views.

These negotiations had to be carried on in conditions of some secrecy, and aroused grave suspicion among strict supporters of Chalcedon and the *Tome*, in East and West. Nevertheless in Rome, where many senators and churchmen were anxious to see Justinian's hand strengthened, and imperial power effectively restored, some concessions were made to a greater understanding of St Cyril's views. His third letter to Nestorius, intended to express the common teaching of Rome and Alexandria, but criticized in Syria and treated with reserve in Rome, was cited as an authority by Pope

John II, who in 533 was prepared to say that 'One of the Trinity, the Son of God himself, suffered in the flesh',[22] despite some murmurings against Theopaschites. But Pope Agapetus, when he came to Constantinople in 535–6, detected heretical tendencies in the Patriarch Anthimus, who had to be deposed to satisfy him, and insisted on steps being taken to establish a Chalcedonian patriarch at Alexandria. The Monophysite patriarch there, Theodosius, whose views were moderate and conciliatory, was interned at Dercos in Thrace. There he remained from 536 until his death in 567, but his imprisonment recovered him support that might otherwise have been lost to a more intransigent figure, Gainas, who held that Christ's divine-human body was by nature incapable of suffering, and that all his sufferings in the flesh were by way of a miraculous condescension to our condition of sin and suffering, a distinct miracle in each and every case.[23] Theodosius of Alexandria followed Severus, who had been Patriarch of Antioch from 512–18, and continued to claim the see until his death in 538, in objections to this.[24] As they came to formulate their own orthodoxy in opposition to Apollinarianism, Eutychianism and Aphthartodocetism, it became more and more evident that this was in substantial agreement with the distinctions made at Chalcedon between Christ's Godhead and manhood. The difference between them and the Chalcedonians is that they insisted on St Cyril's terms, denouncing those of St Leo, and of St Cyril's Syrian critics, Theodoret and Ibas, as altogether inadequate.

The problem now was to find a Pope who would understand them and rally support for a compromise. Vigilius, the deacon of Agapetus, was a man of considerable intelligence. To him is ascribed a letter of peace to Severus and Theodosius, preserved by a hostile witness, Liberatus, in a Latin translation.[25] The authenticity of this is commonly denied, but I see no reason why he should not have written it, and much reason to believe that it explains the imperial support that he received. The difficulty was that at the time when

Agapetus died in Constantinople in 536 the Ostrogoths were in possession of Rome, and with some support from them another Pope, Silverius, had been elected, who had to be deposed as soon as the imperial armies arrived. Exiled to Lycia, he succeeded in enlisting local support for his claims, and was sent back to Rome with an imperial order to hold an enquiry into the circumstances of his election. The Roman commander on the spot, however, supported Vigilius against him, and a little later he died on the island of Palmaria, where it was said that the deacons of Vigilius refused him proper supplies. He died of hunger, but it is not altogether improbable that he was on hunger strike to secure his own restoration.

This greatly added to the difficulties of Vigilius in working for peace, and further trouble was caused by agitation, specially in Palestine, for and against Origenism. Interest in Origen's speculations had never died, and work that has been done in recent years on spiritual writings of the period shows that some of his views on the pre-existence of souls and the possibility of successive lives were being taken to an extreme.[26] But it is likely that much of the agitation was stirred up by admirers of the biblical exegesis of Theodore of Mopsuestia, who shared his objections to mystical interpretation, and feared the discredit of his commentaries if he was condemned as the real author of Nestorianism.

No doubt some who wished to see this done may have been learned in the theology of Origen and used some of his ideas, but to represent the edict in *Three Chapters* issued by Justinian in 543–5 and in a revised form in 551,[27] as a conspiracy to divert attention from Origenist errors is an absurd simplification. This edict is generally represented in text books of church history as if it were concerned entirely with Nestorian propositions found in Theodore's numerous writings, and with the writings of Theodoret and Ibas against St Cyril. Letters of theirs against him were well known at the time of the Council of Chalcedon, and read there before Theodoret and Ibas were acquitted of heresy. It could therefore be argued that if they were orthodox letters then, they were orthodox now, and that any slight on these particular letters would weaken the authority of another letter read at Chalcedon, St Leo's *Tome*. To this it could be objected that the Council of Chalcedon had accepted three letters of St Cyril and one of St Leo as standards of orthodoxy before any definition was framed, but this could not be said of every other letter read there and not censured. The letter of Ibas was not on the same level as St Leo's *Tome*.

But the edict in *Three Chapters* contained, at any rate in its final form, a great deal more, a very careful consideration of the use of theological language, and of the contexts and circumstances in which 'One nature of the incarnate Word', 'Of two natures', and 'In two natures', could legitimately be used.[28] If it had been generally accepted in 545–7, it is not inconceivable that the Monophysite schism could have been healed. But during the delays that preceded the assembly of the Fifth Ecumenical Council in 553, the Monophysites in Syria began to organize a rival hierarchy. Before the Empress Theodora died of cancer in 547, her Monophysite friends had lost patience with the progress of negotiation. One of them, John of Ephesus, was allowed to evangelize pagans in the highlands of Asia Minor on the condition that all four Councils were commemorated in the churches of his foundation. Another, Jacob Baradai, was allowed to go as a missionary bishop to Arethas, king of the Ghassanids, a friendly tribe on the Arabian frontier. From 550 onwards he began to slip in and out of imperial territory on ordination raids, laying hands on priests and deacons, and where he could meet Egyptian bishops to consecrate with him, on bishops. The schism began to establish itself.

Meanwhile Vigilius was brought to Constantinople in 548 in preparation for a Council which he finally refused to attend, but whose decisions he accepted to get his passage home, after his name had been removed from the diptychs, the intercessions for the Pope and the other patriarchs, in the church of Constantinople. The story has been told again and again to his discredit and Justinian's. Justinian was dealing with him much as he did with moderate Monophysite leaders such as Theodosius of Alexandria. So long as they were in restraint and had the appearance of suffering at the hands of the government because of their staunch resistance, they had a reasonable chance of retaining the loyalty of their followers, whatever they did or said. In the wilderness they were bound to oppose the government all the time and the whole way. If they appeared to surrender completely, they would lose all support, but they could claim to have made a good bargain.

Vigilius, as his many pronouncements show, agreed in substance with Justinian. He could see ways in which the edict in *Three Chapters* could be improved, by a more selective treatment of Theodore of Mopsuestia, and by a different way of describing the situation of Theodoret and Ibas at Chalcedon.[29] The Pope and the Emperor do not seem to have disagreed about the positive statements on theological language, which received little attention at the time. The Pope had to appear as leader of resistance to a sell-out until the last moment. Otherwise most people in the West would say that he had been intruded into Rome, at the expense of Silverius, to betray and church to Monophysitism, understood in the sense of Eutychianism.

In fact there was a schism, but a limited one, in some north Italian dioceses. Rome remained in communion with the churches of the East and accepted five Ecumenical Councils.[30] Monophysites were not reconciled, but Monophysite strength came to be limited to Egypt and the African lands beyond it, Armenia, and the outlying parts of Syria. Those who were really offended by the Fifth Ecumenical Council were the Mesopotamian Syrians, who resented the condemnation of three great Syrian doctors, but some of them, like Henana of Nisibis, were prepared to criticize Theodore of Mopsuestia and to look benevolently on Byzantine views.[31]

The Fifth Ecumenical Council has had a bad reputation for three reasons. It put the papacy in an extremely awkward position, which Ultramontanes found humiliating and hard to explain. On the other hand the kind of Protestant who took an interest in church history in the seventeenth and eighteenth centuries was naturally inclined to sympathize with those who defended the first four Councils, including Chalcedon, against innovations of the sixth century. Protestant sympathies were therefore with the schism of Aquileia against Pope Pelagius I, the successor of Vigilius, who had to deal with it with as much prudence as he might, having himself been involved in the opposition to the *Three Chapters*.[32] Then in the nineteenth century the Liberal Protestant historians of dogma, who did so much for the study of church history, admired Paul of Samosata, Marcellus, Eustathius, St Athanasius as the ally of Marcellus and Eustathius, Theodore of Mopsuestia, Nestorius, and Theodoret and Ibas as his allies, but not Origen. They tended to swallow the story of an Origenist conspiracy in favour of mystical interpretation, which they loathed.

And everyone, Catholic and Protestant, was inclined to lose interest in Byzantine history after the fall of the Western Roman Empire in the fifth century. St Leo and the Council of Chalcedon are part of the story of Western Europe. Justinian is not; his reconquest of Italy looks like an interruption between the Ostrogoths, who ruled there from 489 to 536 and in places until 553, and the Lombards who came into north Italy in 568. In fact Justinian restored Rome's Eastern contacts which remained important until the twelfth century. Greek and Syrian influence on Western theology was important in the seventh century and again in the ninth. Greek monasteries in Italy and Sicily continued to multiply in the tenth and eleventh centuries.

☆ **6** ☆

The Dyothelite Controversy

Attempts to heal the Monophysite schism continued after
553. They have never completely ceased, and at the present
day the prospects of success seem better than they have ever
been before.[1] On the side of the Chalcedonians, it must be
said that since 553 they have been prepared to recognize the
orthodoxy of Monophysite terminology, while insisting that
those who will not recognize the orthodoxy of any other
must be treated as heretics. Severus and other Monophysite
leaders were condemned for their judgment on 'in two
natures' in the *Tome* of St Leo and the definitions, as Theodoret and Ibas were condemned for their judgments on St
Cyril and his letters, but not in such strong terms, since their
personal orthodoxy had been recognized at Chalcedon, and
safeguarded in the language of the Fifth Ecumenical Council.
Among the Monophysite groups the Armenians have always
been the most flexible on the theological issues, more concerned with their own identity and uses,[2] the Copts the most
convinced that the terms used by St Athanasius and St Cyril,
Dioscorus, Timothy Aelurus and Theodosius, must be
superior to any others.

The short period between the recovery of Syria from the
Persians by Heraclius in 626–8 and its final loss to the Arabs
in 635–40, is marked by the emergence of successive formularies intended to bridge the gulf by finding positive
expressions of faith with which all parties agreed. When
these proved so controversial that they caused further
trouble, their use was forbidden, but so were attacks upon

them. The Maronites of the Lebanon, who continued to be called Monothelites by their critical neighbours, both Orthodox and Monophysite, even after they had made their peace with Rome in the Middle Ages, were never committed to defending the formulary of 'one will in Christ', proposed by Pope Honorius I as a way of peace between one and two 'energies' and accepted by the Jacobite Patriarch of Antioch, Athanasius the Camel-driver.[3] Their loyalty was rather to the *Type*, the ban on controversy about it. They were not Monothelites, but they saw in Dyothelitism, the doctrine of two wills in Christ, a dangerous doctrine, undermining any possibility of reconciliation, advanced by an original and powerful theologian, without sufficient support in tradition.

The Dyothelite question was most persistently pressed by Maximus, an imperial secretary with a distinguished mind and a thorough philosophical education, who had left the civil service to become a monk, most probably in 613–14, certainly long before the controversy began.[4] The Dyothelite controversy as conducted by him from 640 to his death in lonely exile in 662 was contemporary with the Arab conquest of Syria, Egypt and Libya and of the Persian Empire. Direct references to Islam are rare in his works, but there may be more than have generally been detected if Patricia Crone and Michael Cook are right in reconstructing the history of *Hagarism*, for there are many references to the Jews.

I am sure that their new book with this title, published by the Cambridge University Press in 1977, will receive severe criticism and will not emerge unscathed. I think myself that in their account of the Christian communities under Islam they are inclined to take leaps from the ninth century to the modern period when more information is available. But I am sure that they are right in calling attention to a number of Christian accounts of Muhammad and his movement in conflict with the traditions of Islam. Some of these clearly took shape before the Koran was written down.[5] In these the prophet proclaims the advent of the Messiah in the near future; he himself claims to hold the keys of the kingdom of heaven like Peter; and he is alive at the time of the conquest of Palestine. In the Islamic tradition the second caliph, Umar, has the title of *al-faruq*, the redeemer. Was he at one time, and by some people, regarded as the promised Messiah? Evidence in an Armenian chronicle that may not be quite so early as Crone and Cook suppose[6] represents Muhammad as persuading Arabs to accept their relationship as descendants of Abraham with a number of Jewish refugees who had fled into the wilderness after Heraclius recovered Edessa from the Persians in 628. Muhammad organized them into an army with units corresponding to the twelve tribes of Israel, and set out to recover Palestine for the children of Abraham.

The time and place of this are manifestly wrong.[7] The movement must have begun before 628, and many Jews were in Arabia already, but it is in line with an early Muslim text, the *Constitution of Medina*, in pointing to a time when the Jews there formed a single community with the followers of the prophet.[8] In what came to be the canonical Muslim tradition the prophet and his disciples have left Mecca for Medina and returned to the holy shrine where Abraham sacrificed his son. But this shrine was recovered and restored at Jerusalem. No one who has been in the Dome of the Rock will doubt that the object of those who built it was to expose and venerate a holy spot older than the Temple of Solomon, older than Melchizedek and Abraham, the true navel and centre of the earth. Umar, who did this in the first place, if those who followed made the shrine more and more magnificent, must have been seen at the time as the Messianic restorer of Jerusalem. But the Jews would not participate in this restoration. They turned against the attempt that was being made to reverse the role of Jew and Arab. In such places as Yemen, and in parts of Ethiopia, Jewish kings had reigned over other Semitic tribes and acknowledged some kinship between them and Israel. But to set up an Ishmaelite ruler, with a new revelation given to a prophet in Arabia, over a chosen people of Ishmaelites and Israelites, was quite another matter. When the Jews finally rejected this, another interpretation of Islamic origins had to be constructed, with pilgrimage to Abraham's shrine at Mecca, not at Jerusalem.[9] The protection extended to Jews as 'people of the book' remained, and was applied to Christians, whose numbers in Mesopotamia as well as in Egypt and Syria made it important to conciliate them. But Arabs at the beginning of their conquests were pro-Jewish and anti-Christian.

A passage in a letter of Maximus, assigned by Polycarp Sherwood to 634–40[10] gives some support to this interpretation. He speaks of a race 'eremical and wild' coming in from the wilderness and occupying the fields of others as their own, having the face and forms of men. He goes on to speak of the Jewish people rejoicing in this work of destruction. The implication seems to be that the Jews see in this movement the work of their own one God, breaking down idolatrous representations of him, and preparing the way for their own return in triumph, but Maximus sees it as the work of anti-Christ, establishing himself in the holy place. In the years that followed this no doubt stimulated his enquiry into what is distinctive in the Christian tradition, into the essential differences between the Old and New Testaments.

Maximus has been described as a trenchant critic of Origen and Origenism, but his questions were nearer Origen's than any that had been raised in the Arian and christological controversies.[11] His level of concern is one that he had in common with Origen and with the unknown author of the writings ascribed to Dionysius the Areopagite. In Origen movement is a consequence of the fall, of souls stepping out of line, and so losing their place in the eternal dance. Christ alone moved, but did not fall, in search of others who erred, and must be redeemed. In Maximus movement or action is a fundamental quality in every creature. Each has its own meaning and purpose, reflecting the eternal and divine Logos through whom all things were made. All creatures have a goal to which they move. But man is the image of the divine Logos and the purpose of his nature is to develop his likeness to God. In life as a whole man's role is to unify all things in God and to overcome the evil powers of separation, division, disintegration and death. The 'natural', created movement and energy of man, his will and purpose, is directed towards communion with God, not in isolation from the rest of creation, but as leading everything back to its original state.

For Maximus, as for Origen, freedom is the essential characteristic of man, what makes him different from other animals. In Origen's thought the true perfection of man is out of this world, in the wheel, in the due order of the dance. To Maximus, following St Gregory of Nyssa, true human freedom does not consist of an independent human life, but of the situation truly natural to man, of communion with God.[12] But each individual person also possesses a personality of his or her own, a 'gnomic will', belonging 'to each man as distinct from other men'.

'Christ being God by nature willed what his God and Father wanted, for he shared the will of his own Father,' . . . but 'being man by nature he also willed by nature what is human, but guarding his attention (*oikonomia*), pure of all fantasy, he willed nothing contrary to the Father's will. For nothing that is natural, nor nature herself in her original being, is ever opposed to the ground of nature; not even *gnome* and what comes from it are, in so far as they are in accordance with the law of nature.'[13]

The nature of man supposes communion with God and a direction to good. This Christ took in his human nature. He was naturally human and naturally divine. What he did not have was a human hypostasis with a particular individual will of his own at the centre of his personality. Sin is always a personal action, that does not corrupt human nature as such. The Word could assume the fullness of human nature, but not a 'gnomic' will, ignorant, hesitant, and in conflict with itself. Spiritual life, the life in Christ, supposes the transformation of our individual gnomic will into a 'divine and angelic *gnome*',[14] for our nature's participation in the divine nature is not compatible with the inner conflict introduced into human nature by the devil through the way of the personal 'gnomic' will, of conflict between individuals, beginning with tension between Eve and Adam; but unfallen man was meant to be master of the world. The purpose of redemption was to restore human nature to communion with God in accordance with its own original nature. In an important sense the incarnation continues through the whole history of mankind. The grace of our Lord Jesus Christ works in our human nature through our natural faculties of knowledge to bring the gifts of the Spirit to those who have faith in Christ and open themselves out to communion with him.[15]

This way of looking at the human situation involves distinctions between our natural knowledge of God, the divine Spirit that works in us to develop this knowledge, and the individual, the 'gnomic' will and intellect. This has some relation to the distinctions drawn in the standard commentaries on Aristotle since Alexander of Aphrodisias (*c.* AD 200) between the possible, the habitual, and the active intellect. As we shall see in the next lecture,[16] the active intellect is common to all mankind. It works on the possible intellect, already present in new-born babies, to produce habitual intellects in individuals. It would seem that for standard Syrian commentators on Aristotle, both Monophysite and Nestorian or East Syrian, the human intellect of Christ, with the whole of his human nature, belonged, like the active intellect, to all mankind. Through participation in this we attain to the life of the resurrection. This cannot be confused with Apollinarianism, where the Word of God takes the place of the *nous*, the higher intellect in Christ, nor does Maximus deny that Christ had a 'gnomic will', and an intellect in *habitu*, making judgments from day to day, but this was so perfectly formed by the active intellect as the possible intellect of his infancy 'increased in wisdom and stature' (Luke 2.52), that there was no place for sin in it.

It is clear that Monophysite and Monothelite enemies regarded Maximus as a kind of Nestorian. It is also interesting that the Nestorian, the East Syrian Catholicos Iso

Yahb III in a letter written probably as his campaign was beginning, shows that he was under the impression that Rome, with Ravenna and all Italy, the Franks, Africa, with many Palestinians and Phoenicians, had lately swung over to defending two qualities and operations in Christ.[17] This may be a misunderstanding of the imperial *ekthesis* of 638, disapproving disputes over one or two energies, and commending one will in Christ, a formula that the East Syrians could accept, but it may well be rather later, and refer to the defence of duality in Christ in Africa, Rome and Ravenna by Maximus and the Palestinian Pope Theodore (642–9), and to the kind of concern that this aroused in Monophysite circles on both sides of the traditional border between Rome and Persia, where resurgent Nestorianism in Jerusalem and in Africa and Rome would be denounced, to the great satisfaction of the East Syrians.

In fact Maximus does not seem to have been critical of the *ekthesis* of 638, condemning controversy over one or two energies.[18] He was not an intransigent Chalcedonian, always watching for any concession to the Monophysites, as Sophronius of Jerusalem may have been.[19] But he agreed with Pope John IV, who was probably the original author[20] of the letter of Honorius I, that the formula of peace proposed in this in terms of a unity of will in Christ, was being misused to denounce any idea of two wills in him. When controversy over this was forbidden in the imperial *Type* of 648, he joined Pope Theodore in stirring up trouble against it. By the time of the Lateran Council of 649 Martin I had succeeded Theodore, and he was equally adamant, even more closely associated with Maximus, who was in Rome at the time, although his name does not appear in the Council's proceedings.

At the imperial court this no doubt seemed to be another of the recurrent Roman protests against compromise with the Monophysites. These were hard to suppress, and harder now than they had been a century before, since the balance of power in Italy between the Roman Empire and the Lombards gave the Roman church more freedom of action, but something had to be done to show that the authorities in Constantinople meant to be obeyed in Italy. Pope Martin and Maximus were therefore arrested after some considerable difficulties, and brought to Rome to be tried for treason committed in the course of resistance to their arrest.

Everything possible was done to keep the question of doctrine out of their trial, lest this should excite sympathy in Constantinople for a great theologian with a growing reputation as a spiritual counsellor, and for the primate of the Elder Rome. In fact the Roman resistance, though real, was not very formidable. The Romans had no objection to electing another Pope while Martin was in exile. They could not in fact get on without one, for the Pope was now chief magistrate of Rome. They did not want him to accept a formulary sent from Constantinople as a condition of his recognition,[21] but they did not demand the restoration of Martin or the release of Maximus. The next Pope, Vitalian, who succeeded Eugenius (654–7), was certainly in the diptychs at Constantinople. He received the Emperor Constans II, the author of the *Type*, on a visit to Rome, but his name was removed in 670, probably as a result of controversy in the church and city of Constantinople in which critics of the official policy had appealed to Rome. Of this we know little or nothing, but it cannot have owed much to instigation from Rome in the course of its development, as in the years from 670 to 677 the Arabs were in command of the seas, including much of the Aegean, and communications between Constantinople and Rome were very difficult indeed.[22]

It is clear that there were Monothelites, especially Macarius, Patriarch of Antioch, who were concerned to keep the lines open to those who were still resisting the Arabs, including Armenians and Mardaites in the Lebanon who wanted to be assured that Chalcedon was not being taken in a Nestorian or in a strictly Western sense, with no terms but those of the *Tome*, but the Dyothelite concern was a different one. Maximus and Pope Martin were represented as hardline

Chalcedonians, but their real concern was with divine energy and human free will in Christ. This appears in the final definition of the Sixth Ecumenical Council of 681, which for the Eastern Orthodox is more important as a theological starting point than the definition of Chalcedon or the more balanced determination of 553, although the irreformability of these is taken for granted in it.

In 681 the names of Martin and Maximus were not mentioned. Much attention was paid to problems of balance in deciding which heretics from what patriarchates were to be condemned. Not too many patriarchs of Constantinople were to be classed as Monothelites, but one Pope must be with patriarchs of Alexandria and Antioch and one bishop from the patriarchate of Jerusalem. But the definition shows the influence of Maximus in its confidence and clarity:

'We believe that he who is one of the Holy Trinity and after the incarnation our Lord Jesus Christ is our true God: we say that his double nature shone forth through his single hypostasis, wherein he displayed his miracles and his sufferings through the entire course of his mission, not in appearance only but in truth, because of the distinction of the natures in one and the same hypostasis, where (in communion with one another) each nature wills and does what is proper to it. Therefore we confess two wills and two energies concurring for the salvation of man.'[23]

This became the starting point for later discussions of the divine energy and operation in the Byzantine world. The basis of the definition is that Christ participated equally in the divine nature and energy and in the freedom of the human will. While it is related to the Nestorian and Monophysite controversies there is a new element in it that has more to do with the challenge of Islam. To this the reply of Maximus is 'Let us become gods through the Lord, because for this did man exist; being by nature God and Lord.'[24] He saw the doctrine of the Trinity as a mean between extremes of monism and polytheism.

Maximus is as important for the East as St Augustine for

the West. In three respects they are similar characters. Both were philosophic minds who left behind them no comprehensive systematic treatise, but a great deal of work implying a coherent personal view of the world, enough to fascinate followers who perhaps read into it more than was there. Both contributed by selection to the preservation of Greek philosophy and psychology, St Augustine by his reading and use of the Neo-Platonists, Maximus by his critical reading of Origen and the Origenists and of the Dionysian writings with notes that he preserved and enlarged. Thirdly they contended against adversaries who can hardly be called heresiarchs. The Pelagians said what most ordinary preachers and moralists say, and St Augustine exposed its superficiality. Those who built up the monergistic and Monothelite 'watery union'[25] were not inventing a heresy but papering over cracks with a formula of peace that St Maximus ruthlessly tore down.

St John of Damascus, a much tidier mind than St Maximus, made a text book out of him which had a vast influence, because it was put together by a trained administrator. But he was not an original mind. He was a Maximist, who shared the same concerns with Islam and Judaism, with the understanding of the Dionysian writings, and in a secondary way with Monothelites, Monophysites and Nestorians as immediate neighbours, as well as with contemporary controversies about the use and abuse of images. The West knew Maximus as a commentator on Dionysius, translated by John the Scot, who also translated some of his other works, but they fell into some discredit when John the Scot did, and when Eastern theology was suspected in the Middle Ages. He is only now beginning to be rediscovered.[26]

7

Christians under Muslim Rule

In the first two centuries after the consolidation of Islam as a religion and as an imperial power the Caliphate of the Ommayads at Damascus from 660–754, and of the Abbasids at Baghdad in the century after, used the administrative methods and imitated the coins of their predecessors, and so were obliged to employ their civil servants. In Syria, Egypt and Libya these were generally Christians. In Mesopotamia and Persia under the Sassanids they had included a Christian element, as well as Chaldean pagans, under Zoroastrian superiors. Under Islam the Zoroastrians were not privileged but proscribed. The Christians were free to convert them, and to convert the Chaldeans, and they often did, while others became Muslims. The East Syrians or Nestorians were accustomed to live under an alien government. They had long provided doctors as well as traders and some administrators in the Persian Empire. They now had a stronger hold, since Zoroastrian institutions of religious education collapsed and Chaldean were restricted. They found themselves conducting education not only in medicine but in astronomy, and their schools of philosophy were used increasingly outside their own community.

The Syrian Monophysites, now called Jacobites, who were found among them as well as in Roman Syria, also contained an educated element who welcomed the Muslim conquest to this extent, that they were now free from fear of a return to discrimination in favour of the Chalcedonians. On the other hand much of their strength lay in Arabian tribes such as the

Ghassanids, and in frontier villages on the edge of the wilderness where Islam was quick to gain ground. The Monophysite Copts in Egypt had some of the same difficulties. On the one hand they retained a share in the day to day administration of a country whose problems only Egyptians understand. This they had never lost. The Byzantines could not have ruled Egypt without some co-operation outside Chalcedonian circles. The Arabs made more use of the Copts, who still had a lot of minor administrative jobs at the beginning of the present century. But many of their disciples in the oases were attracted to Islam by the very simplicity and regularity of its rituals, which can be performed without any use of corn or wine, simply by prayer and prostration.

The Armenians and the Mardaites of Mount Lebanon[1] were the most stout in resistance to invasion, and the most persistent in believing that some concerted Christian resistance could and should be maintained. After 681 when the Byzantines abandoned the idea of any attempt to rebuild an alliance with the Jacobites, the disciples of Sophronius and Maximus, chiefly in Palestine, became Melkites, the Emperor's men, identified with Byzantine Orthodoxy, and subject to greater difficulties than others, but they did not disappear, and under the Ommayads at Damascus played a part in the administration there. At the time of the surrender of the city they had been in opposition to the policy of the Emperor. The Al-Mansur family were said to have opened the gates.[2] In the eighth century they provided the Caliph with an administrative secretary, John, who later retired to the monastery of St Sabbas, south of Jerusalem, and became a systematic theologian.

The theology of St John of Damascus was extensively used as a textbook afterwards in the Byzantine church. It was translated into Latin by Burgundio of Pisa in the twelfth century, and used in the *Sentences* of Peter Lombard as well as in the *Summa Theologiae* of St Thomas Aquinas. It reflects the education of the civil service in the Caliphate at Damascus, following models long established in the Roman and Persian Empires.[3]

Education for the service developed on the lines of the classical education of the municipal aristocracies in the Hellenistic world and in the Roman Empire. The *trivium* consisted of three main subjects, grammar, the study of literary language and its correct pronunciation, developed through the study and composition of verses, rhetoric, the art of expression, originally in terms of oratory, but in the later Roman Empire in terms of a well-expressed letter, and dialectic, the art of logical argument. To these were added as subordinate subjects the *quadrivium*, arithmetic, geometry, astronomy and music. This had been a Greek and Latin education, and uniform with at most differences of emphasis from one end of the Roman Empire to the other, but as the knowledge of Greek declined in the West, educational handbooks, including translations of Greek texts, began to appear in Latin. At about the same time or a little earlier began the translation of Aristotle's *Organon* into Syriac.[4]

This is associated with the schools of Edessa and with Probha or Probus, said to have been archdeacon and archiatros, head of the medical faculty at Antioch, a Greek city where many of the people spoke Syriac, and a contemporary of Ibas, Bishop of Edessa at the time of the Nestorian controversy, who died in 457. The schools of Edessa had a larger proportion of Syriac-speaking students, many of whom wanted to learn Greek in order to understand the New Testament and the Christian Fathers, especially the commentaries of Diodore of Tarsus, Theodore of Mopsuestia, and Theodoret. In 489 an important group of lecturers, discontented with the concessions made by the Byzantine Government to Egyptian and Syrian opposition to Chalcedon, moved to Nisibis, on the other side of the Persian frontier. We know more about schools there[5] which were evidently institutions of the church, whereas at Edessa we may presume that they trained civil servants as well as potential preachers. But at both there were medical schools, with text books whose original language was Greek, and certainly schools of logic.

An introduction to the study of the scriptures by an African layman called Junilius, written in Latin for an African bishop who had come to Constantinople for the Fifth General Council, is based on a similar text book by Paul the Persian, who taught at Nisibis.[6] From this we gather that the scripture course there distinguished between the canonical scriptures and the *antilegomena*, of middle authority, including Job, Esther, Wisdom, the Song of Songs, the Epistle of St James, II Peter, II John, and the Apocalypse. Not very long after this Henana, a teacher at Nisibis, got into trouble for including Job in his lecture course.[7] It is clear that the lectures presumed some knowledge of the terms used, not only in the *Organon* of Aristotle, but in the commentaries of Porphyry on this. The students had been through an introductory course of logic.

At Nisibis it was possible to do this without Greek. Translations of the *Isagoge* of Porphyry, the *Categories* of Aristotle, and tracts on the soul are attributed to Sergius of Reshaina, who came from a Monophysite background in Syria, but seems to have fallen out with Severus and attached himself to the Patriarch Ephraim of Antioch, who sent him to Constantinople to see Pope Agapetus in 535–6. They both died there in the same year. His works were dedicated to his friend Theodore, who became East Syrian Metropolitan of Merv, and would be counted a Nestorian by Monophysites and some Chalcedonians, but they also used the works of Sergius, at any rate on secular subjects. A Syriac manuscript in the British Museum includes tracts on logic, on negation and affirmation, and 'On the causes of the universe, according to the view of Aristotle, showing how it is a circle', with another tract on the action and influence of the moon, which has an appendix on the motion of the sun.[8]

So far as I know, these have never been published,[9] but I think it would be profitable for a Syriac scholar to compare 'On the causes of the universe according to the views of

Aristotle', with the *Liber de causis* ascribed to Aristotle himself, and translated into Latin in the twelfth century. Of this Etienne Gilson says in his *History of Christian Philosophy in the Middle Ages*: 'The origins of the *De causis* are still obscure, but that of its content is clear.' It comes from Plotinus through Proeclus. The Arabian Aristotle was 'a mixture of Aristotle and Plotinus'.[10] This mixture was made and stirred in the Syrian schools.

These were church schools developing a classical curriculum for use not only by preachers and teachers, but by medical men and an increasing number of other public servants who had to work, not in the Christian society of the Byzantine Empire, but in the Persian Empire, officially Zoroastrian, and then under the Caliphate. In the Byzantine Empire itself there were distinctions between government schools, preparing for the civil service, and the schools of the church, which claimed a monopoly of theology. At Nisibis the theology was an important part of the course, and other branches of study developed in accordance with theological preoccupations, not only concerned with the controversy between the East Syrians and Jacobites who called them Nestorian, but with apologetic against the official religion, Zoroastrianism, and against Chaldean astrology.

We are told of a Jacobite Metropolitan of Tagrith of Armenian origin, consecrated in 559, Ahu-dh'emmeh, that he wrote on logic, on free will, on the composition of man as consisting of soul and body, and on man as microcosm of the world, a favourite theme with Maximus, who may well have derived it from the same or similar sources.[11] Paul the Persian, whose introduction to the scriptures was adapted to Junilius to Western needs, also wrote an introduction to the dialectics of Aristotle. A little later a *periodeutes*, a kind of archdeacon, called Bodh, not only wrote a kind of encylopaedia on 'Greek Questions', but translated a collection of Indian stories, that afterwards went the rounds of medieval popular literature under the title of Kalila and Dimna.[12] This interest in India was extended by Severus Sebokht of Nisibis,

who afterwards became a Jacobite bishop in Western Syria,
to geography and astronomy. He commented on the excel-
lence of Indian calculations, and in this connections made
reference to their nine signs. He also wrote a treatise on the
astrolabe.[13] According to Assemani he was a bishop in the
time of the Jacobite Patriarch Athanasius the Camel-driver
(631–48), a teacher probably earlier.[14] He probably gained
his knowledge of Indian numerals before the Arab conquests.

Not long after the medical school at Jundishapur, which
was certainly flourishing in Sassanid times, possessed an
observatory with a fine collection of astronomical instruments. I would suggest that one of the achievements of Christian medical science in Syria and Mesopotamia was a kind
of secularization of astrology, and that to this a knowledge
of Indian and Chinese observations may have contributed.
For the Chaldeans the observations of the stars was one of
the traditional ways of worshipping the gods. The heavenly
powers are truly divine, and their influence on our sublunary
sphere must be observed, but not criticized or defied. Jews
and Christians saw the stars and planets with other heavenly
beings as creatures of immense antiquity and refined spirituality, but like the angels subject to temptation, and like
devils overruled by the same divine providence that makes
our perverse purposes instruments of his will. Astrological
influences are real and natural, but not inexorable.

Astronomy and alchemy had a larger part in the Babylonian curriculum than they generally had in the Byzantine,
because the influence of the Chaldean astrologers was so
persistent, and continued under Islam. The *Metaphysics* of
Aristotle was also useful in Zoroastrian days to provide
apologetic for the unity of the cosmos, and continued part
of the curriculum. The Syrian Aristotle was evidently larger
than the Byzantine, and much larger than the Latin Aristotle
of the early Middle Ages, before new Latin translations were
made from the Arabic in Spain. To these the Byzantines
added some corrected versions,[15] but they were chiefly useful
in detecting the differences between the real and the Arabian

Aristotle.[16] I would suggest that the Arabian Aristotle, including the *Liber de causis*, was substantially Syrian, and that the Syrian *quadrivium* on mathematics and astronomy included Indian and Chinese materials.

In the first two centuries after the Arab conquest references to schools and problems of school management multiply in East Syrian ecclesiastical history. Monks resented the presence of students and disliked being turned into schoolmasters. Concessions had to be made to their needs, but the schools continued. Under the Abbasid Caliphs, who shifted the capital to Baghdad after 754, the number of Muslim students of arts and medicine were increasing, but as yet they had no masters and schools of their own. They came to Christian schools. The Christians had long been accustomed to deal with a situation in which the most dangerous thing that could happen was the conversion of a Zoroastrian student, the son of a ruler. For this reason they had always taken care to avoid any preaching in school, and to make their arguments for the unity of God philosophical, turning on reason, not on revelation. But no doubt many of their Muslim students came from families with a Christian background who had lately become Muslim in order to rise in the world. More of these students would have come back to the church in the Christian atmosphere of the schools if some Muslim scholars had not devised arguments to help them. The Mutazilites[17] were especially concerned to establish the absolute unity of God, and the justice of the divine will. They denied that good was good and evil evil only because God had willed them to be such, refusing to allow any distinction between God's essence and his attributes. In their line of argument we can see an assertion that Islam, not Christianity, is consistently monotheistic, and can be purged of all idolatry, of any anthropomorphism in the representation of the divine.

A kind of natural theology emerges from this debate, which is common ground between Christians, Muslims and Jews. The first Muslim philosopher whose writings are preserved is Alkindi, who lived at Basra and Baghdad and died in 873. His writings cover the whole field of Greek learning, but Gilson pays special attention to a tract on the intellect, which could be related to one on the soul, ascribed to Aristotle but not the *De anima*, in the translations of Sergius of Reshaina. Gilson notes that Alkindi claims to be following Plato and Aristotle in regarding 'the intellect always in act' as a spiritual being or substance superior to the individual soul, and acting on it so as to turn a possible intellect into 'a soul intelligent in act'.[18] Gilson connects this with the influence of Alexander of Aphrodisias on all subsequent commentaries on Aristotle, and no one would want to deny this, but I would suggest that the idea of one agent intellect for all mankind, turning potency into action in our lives, came to the Arabs from Syrian Christians who saw it in the context of christology. The agent intellect was the humanity that Christ took, common to all mankind, and to be risen with him is to participate in the fullness of this. Without christology this common intellect becomes an abstraction, but the idea caught on in the West afterwards because its reference to the Second Man was perceived.

Alkindi was probably not an original thinker. Al-Farabi in the next generation (870–950) came from Transoxiana, and learnt his logic from a Christian teacher in Baghdad. A recent Muslim writer, Seyyed Hossein Nasr, expounds his system of education, leading through the *trivium* and *quadrivium*, developed to include optics, weights and tool-making for astronomy and music, to physics and metaphysics. Metaphysics is defined as 'the knowledge of incorporal beings, their qualities and characteristics, leading finally to the knowledge of the Truth, that is of God, one of whose names is Truth'.[19] The early Muslim philosophers stress their debt to the Christian Honain-ibq Ishaq (810–873), physician to the Caliph Al-Mutawakkil. He had been to Byzantium and had studied there in the age of Leo of Salonica, who led a revival of learning at Constantinople in 847–67.[20]

But in the century that followed the unity of the Muslim

world began to break up, and learning survived in its out-
posts, in Bactria and Spain, better than at the centre, in Syria
and Mesopotamia. Moreover Islam as a religion rejected the
philosophical approach to theology, not unanimously, but in
general. This lingered in circles of intellectuals patronized by
particular emirs. In the East there was still a good deal of
common ground between Muslim and Christian scholars,
who read each other's books. The last Syriac summaries of
knowledge in the thirteenth century owe much to Muslim
philosophers. Gregory Bar-Hebraeus translated Avicenna
into Syriac.[21] But while this was lost, with much, perhaps
most Syriac philosophy and secular literature, which ceased
to be copied as Syriac ceased to be a spoken language, and
now lingers only in libraries, the influence of Arabian philosophy on Latin scholasticism was immense.

This is partly because the Muslim and Jewish scholars
whom the Latins encountered in Spain while the curriculum
of the University of Paris was in process of formation, were
not very orthodox Muslims or generally very orthodox Jews.
They were not a danger to their own orthodoxy as a subtle
Greek or oriental Christian might have been, and they had
an interpretation of Plato and Aristotle, the philosophers
who had always been part of a general education in arts, in
terms that were not distinctive of any religion.[22] They saw
these as the terms of a natural theology, acceptable to Gen-
tiles, which in the Middle Ages generally means Jews and
Muslims, as well as to Christians. But this has little to do
with the religion of 'the wild man in the woods'[23] in whose
problems St Thomas Aquinas was also interested. It is very
much the product of a particular culture or set of cultures,
and not of man's natural condition.

An example may be found in Avicenna's treatment of the
heavenly bodies.[24] He holds that they must have intelligences
to steer them on their courses, since they move in circles. If
they were simply material bodies they would go straight on
or fall down. What keeps them in motion is love for the
central intelligence around whom they revolve. There is an

element here from Chaldean astronomy, but also from the *Celestial Hierarchies* of Dionysius the Areopagite,[25] and other earlier visions of the heavenly dance, Babylonian, Christian and Neo-Platonic. Natural theology has a history. It arises out of concerns that recur wherever religions learn from one another.

8

The Impact of the Crusades

It could be said that the Crusading movement began in the south of France and Spain. *The Song of Roland* is an epic poem of Charlemagne's battle with the Moors, written at the time of the first Crusade. A text composed at St Denis at the time describes him as a Crusader liberating Jerusalem,[1] but the Spanish epic of the Cid deals with a hero who acted as political adviser to the Moorish kings of Saragossa, and became familiar with Muslim politics and law before he liberated Valencia in 1089–97.[2] In Spain over four centuries Muslims and Christians had grown accustomed to one another, as in the East. The educated class, interested in philosophical, scientific and religious problems, included Jews and Christians as well as not very orthodox Muslims. So the Latins enlarged their knowledge of Aristotle and his commentators mainly, though not entirely, from Muslim and Jewish sources in the twelfth and thirteenth centuries, so acquiring a philosophy and theology independent of revelation, which could be taught as a supplement to the dialectic of Aristotle, and represented as natural, human, perennial.

But meanwhile the older sources of communication between the Greek East and the Latin West were becoming blocked. Until the eleventh century Rome and the East were kept in touch largely through the Greek elements in Italy and Sicily, the Latin in Illyricum, Thrace and Constantinople, and pilgrims to Jerusalem. The first had been there before the Christian era and the rise of the Roman Empire, and while their numbers fluctuated, Greek monasteries in Italy were still being founded in the eleventh century, including Grottoferrata, founded by St Neilos of Rossano at the very end of his life in 1004.[3] Conflict and tension between Greek and Latin elements in Southern Italy was in the nature of the case not uncommon, and it had come to be involved in the conflicts of jurisdiction between Rome and the emperor and patriarch of Constantinople. The importance of these however must not be exaggerated. They arose out of an older tension over Illyricum, Greece and the Greek islands, whose bishops did not belong to the patriarchate of Constantinople, at any rate before 732, but when they went to the imperial city on business, naturally called on the patriarch and sat down with other bishops in his home synod.

The Iconoclast emperors incorporated them in the patriarchate and added Sicilian sees and a few in South Italy where they could hope to enforce their policy.[4] They did not attempt to impose it on Rome, Taranto or Naples, but when they failed to enforce it in the body of the Empire, and gave it up, they did not restore the former patriarchal boundaries. No doubt this was resented at Rome, but the issue was not often considered to be of the first importance. So far as Illyricum and Greece were concerned the bishops would have had great difficulty in getting to Rome anyway in the ninth century. The Greek clergy in south Italy and Sicily had a different discipline in such matters as marriage and the length of Lent. This made difficulties when Greeks and Latins were living close to each other, which might be accentuated if there were more Greeks in the suburbican dioceses, Rome's own metropolitan province. So while Rome from time to time continued to protest, she acquiesced, except for a brief moment in the 860s when Pope Nicholas I saw an opportunity to acquire Bulgaria, partly in the old Illyricum, partly in Thrace, for the Western church.[5] This led to conflict, but it would seem also to a practical agreement which put Bulgaria outside the Byzantine patriarchate, but practically autonomous, and open to Greek influence, while Greece and the Greek islands, Sicily, Calabria and Otranto in Apulia, remained in the Byzantine sphere. How far Rome recognized this is not clear, but the Popes of the period, very much absorbed in the local affairs of the *ducatus Romanus*, behaved as if they did.[6]

What changed everything was the Norman conquest of Southern Italy and Sicily, beginning in 1021–3 with the enlistment of Norman soldiers of fortune in local conflicts, and ending by 1071 with the practical extinction of Byzantine government in this area, as well as of Moorish strongholds seized from Africa and held for two hundred years by Berber and Moorish chiefs. The last stages in the Norman conquest of what came to be called the kingdom of the two Sicilies, on the mainland and on the island, were contemporary with the Norman conquest of England. For Normans moving north and south the dominant figure in religious life was the Abbot of Bec, Lanfranc who became Archbishop of Canterbury after 1066.[7] He was a canon lawyer and theologian of note, who had friends in the circle of reformers around the Archdeacon Hildebrand. Hildebrand was becoming a more and more important figure in the affairs of the Roman church from 1049, when he returned from exile to offer his services to Leo IX, the third in a series of reforming popes who came from beyond the Alps, and were imposed on the Roman church by the German Holy Roman Emperor Henry III, until 1073 when he himself became Pope Gregory VII.[8]

One of Hildebrand's most important achievements before he became Pope was the alliance between the Apostolic See and the Normans. This gave to the reforming party in Rome protectors who were not members of the local Roman nobility, and had no imperial claims. On the contrary their claim to a legal title to their conquests in Italy and Sicily, and in other islands, including Britain, depended on their recognition of the claims of the Pope to imperial power in the western regions and islands of the Roman Empire. The Popes of this time had come to take the *Donation of Constantine* seriously. Whatever its origin, probably Roman, the Popes of the ninth century treated it with some caution, while those of the tenth ignored it. It came back to Rome from Germany and Lorraine in the middle of the eleventh century, and became an instrument of Roman diplomacy in regard to the boundaries of the patriarchates and the status of Latin churches in Constantinople.[9]

The Greeks of south Italy and Sicily survived the Norman conquest and in time won favour with their new masters, but they were henceforth a subordinate element, rather than a source of inspiration and learning. The Norman conquest of Sicily created a pattern repeated by the same family in the principality of Antioch in the First Crusade, when they refused to restore the city to the Roman (Byzantine) Empire, and insisted on the ordination of Latin bishops to important sees. Since the Patriarch John would not go on doing this,[10] they enlisted the aid of Daimbert of Pisa, who had just become Patriarch of Jerusalem, and when John retired to Constantinople in indignation, they put in a Latin patriarch of Antioch.

This is a far more important crisis in the relationship of East and West than the trouble in 1051–4 over Latin churches in Constantinople. These were attacked and closed as a reprisal for attacks by the Normans on Greek churches in Italy and Sicily, and this led to a virulent popular controversy, in which lists of errors were developed on both sides.[11] But it was not the beginning of a new schism between Rome and Constantinople. The Pope's name had been missing from the diptychs there for some time, but it was still commemorated in Antioch, Alexandria and Jerusalem, and at Constantinople they were prepared to restore it, if satisfaction were given on some points of doctrine and discipline.[12] This it was difficult to obtain, and more difficult after the Hildebrandine reform of the Western church than it had been on previous occasions,[13] but Rome had always been reluctant to give an account of her faith to anyone else who might implicitly or explicitly accuse her of unorthodoxy. This was the real difficulty about the *filioque*, when once it came to be incorporated in the Roman creed. We do not quite know when this was, but certainly after 1009 and almost certainly some time before 1054, perhaps with the German occupation of Rome in 1046, perhaps earlier.[14]

At the time of the First Crusade there was certainly a will to agreement in which the Emperor, the papal legate, and the Patriarchs of Antioch and Jerusalem were all involved, if the Patriarch of Constantinople was less enthusiastic and disposed to put more hope in the anti-Pope, Clement III, supported by the Germans and the Emperor Henry IV.[15] But the schism at Antioch made everything more difficult. Demands for the restoration of a Greek patriarch were constantly made by the Byzantines, and once succeeded for a short time in the 1160s.[16] But resistance to them not only by the local Latins but in Rome made the Byzantines critical of the intrusion of a Latin patriarch into Jerusalem, and of Latin clergy into the most important of the holy places there. They began to put pressure on their own local Latin churches, and on Latin monasteries in Byzantine territory.[17]

This made for an atmosphere in which Latins who wished to learn of Greek wisdom, pagan and Christian, from Byzantine sources were treated with suspicion. Some of them, like the brother Hugo Etherianus and Leo Tuscus did do a good deal of translating, and attempted eirenical explanations of differences.[18] There were those in the West in the twelfth century who thought that much could be learnt from the Greeks, not only in Sicily but in France.[19] But the current was running against them as the scholastic curriculum was in process of formation. Peter Lombard's *Sentences* included material from St John of Damascus, but otherwise little that was Greek or Eastern. The reputation of John the Scot and of Maximus declined, except in relation to the *Corpus Areopagitum*, which remained authoritative because it was regarded as apostolic.

Then came more trouble between Greeks and Latins at Constantinople in 1182. In the reign of the Byzantine Emperor Manuel I (1143–80) there had been a real possi-

bility that empire and papacy might at last accommodate
their differences. In 1166, with a Greek patriarch in Antioch,
the Pope was pressed to recognize Manuel as Roman
Emperor. He was told that on this condition his name would
be restored to the diptychs, and appeals to Rome from the
decisions of the other patriarchs restored as of old. But Alexander III and his cardinals detected an implication in this
that made for reserve, although negotiations continued.
What Manuel meant by Roman Emperor was emperor of
the old undivided Roman Empire, of which St Gregory the
Great had been a loyal subject, although sometimes dis-
obedient to orders from the court. It was very much more
than an honour bestowed by the Pope on Frankish kings
who came to get benefits from him and to help him in local
difficulties.[20] The Holy Roman Emperor of the moment,
Frederick Barbarossa, was hostile and supported a rival, an
anti-Pope, but he might come round, while a 'translation of
the empire' back from the Germans to the Greeks would
antagonize not only him but all Germans, all Franks, many
Lombards, and might well win the day for the anti-Pope
whom Barbarossa supported. Alexander had to think too of
the kings of England and France. He held up the negotiations,
and in 1177 the ambassadors of Manuel beheld with horror
the submission of Frederick Barbarossa, defeated by the
Lombard cities and in need of the Pope's support.[21] He could
humiliate himself before the Apostolic See and his humilia-
tion could win him victory. But no Roman Emperor from
Byzantium could afford to act as the Pope's groom,[22] and so
admit his right to dispose of such places as Sicily, Corfu and
Antioch.

After Manuel's death in 1180 came the inevitable anti-
Latin reaction in Constantinople and a line-up for and
against the Latins in the Crusading states. There the Crusaders had begun by treating the Orthodox Chalcedonians as
part of the same Catholic community with themselves, and
so they remained at Jerusalem through the whole time of the
Latin occupation from 1099 to 1187. That did not prevent

the Greek monks of Saint Sabbas from receiving Greek and Russian pilgrims.[23] They still had their special place in the Easter ceremonies at the Holy Sepulchre, and they still had a place for monks who sang in Latin, as well as for Greeks, Georgians and Syrians, in their own community from the twelfth to the fifteenth century.[24] But no doubt they and the other local Orthodox, Syrians, Georgians and Greeks alike, resented the Latin monopoly of superior positions, and some aspects of the Latin attitude to Maronites, Armenians and Jacobites.

These were outside the Catholic community, but Armenian relations with it had always been ambivalent. They were more concerned for their own calendar and usages than with objections to Chalcedon.[25] In one of their uses which Greeks and Syrians generally disliked, the matter of *azymes*, unleavened bread, in the eucharist, the Latins actually agreed with them. They also found that in Cilicia and other places the Armenians could provide auxiliary troops, as willing to fight against Greeks as against Turks. The Maronites of Mount Lebanon were archers. Their dim memories of their original divergence from Maximists and Jacobites pointed back to day of heroic resistance to Arab conquest in their mountain strongholds, and to a formula provided by Honorius of Rome. The Franks were prepared to accept their orthodoxy in 1181,[26] but this no doubt exposed them to more Melkite criticism. They also found that some of the Jacobites were ready to be reconciled with Rome on terms that were less demanding than Melkites or Byzantines would require.[27]

No doubt the Franks were written off as ignorant barbarians, unversed in theological subtleties. But by 1180 this could no longer be taken for granted. In the thirteenth century it was certainly not true of the Francisans and Dominicans involved in the affairs of the Eastern churches. It seems much more likely that they had come to recognize the substantial orthodoxy of the Armenians and of other Monophysites, and also of the Nestorian East Syrians. Bar-

Hebraeus in his *Candelabrum Sanctorum* found all the Eastern churches in substantial agreement on the doctrine of the Trinity and the integrity of the Godhead and manhood of Christ. A summary of his argument by Assemani is confirmed by examination of the text.[28] Assemani ascribes a like view of the situation to Elias, the Nestorian Metropolitan of Damascus, writing in the ninth century.[29] Bar-Hebraeus, writing about 1280, was almost certainly influenced by conversation with friars from the West.

The deepest resentment then was not against Latin theological requirements, which were less exacting than those of the Byzantines, but against the demand for submission to a Pope whose position in Christendom was akin to that of the Caliph in Islam, a Pope who was more of an Emperor than the King of France or Frederick Barbarossa or Henry VI, his son. This became crystal clear in the last years of the twelfth century and the first of the thirteenth, when the German throne was in dispute after the death of Henry VI in 1197. The diversion of the Fourth Crusade to Constantinople was not intended or projected by Pope Innocent III, but it was the inevitable consequence of his policies.

In the disputed succession to the imperial throne he had come down on the side of Otto IV of Brunswick. This made it vital to the other candidate, Philip of Swabia, the brother of Henry VI and uncle of his heir, Frederick II, to make the most of his connection with the projected Crusade without running the risk of exiling himself in Palestine. He hoped by restoring his father-in-law Isaac Angelus to the Byzantine throne to accomplish a church union which would please the Pope without going too far off. From Byzantium he could return to Germany at the next opportunity. But Pope Innocent, already enraged at the use the Venetians had made of the Crusade in Dalmatia, and rightly suspicious of Venetian intentions there and in Greece, insisted on another attempt to recover Jerusalem. The Crusaders were told that if they left there would be a rising against their collaborators. The rising actually began. They stayed to put it down, and became involved in the sack of the city and the division of the Empire in 1204.

The Latin Empire of Romania was never more than a loose collection of principalities, something like the string of Frankish principalities down the coast of Syria and Palestine. As these were always hampered by unconquered gaps, so were the Franks in Romania by Greek strongholds independent of one another in Epirus, Nicaea and Trebizond, which gradually consolidated into the Empire that recaptured Constantinople in 1261. The Venetians, who knew what could be held, got by far the most valuable share, and kept a good deal of it, in such places as Crete and Naxos, into the sixteenth century.

All the Frankish states in Greece had Greek subjects, who were treated on the model of government originally worked out in the Holy Land of Palestine, and then applied in Cyprus.[30] But whereas in Palestine the Greeks and the Christian Syrians began by regarding the Crusaders as friends, and gradually came to see them as oppressors and conquerors, in Cyprus, acquired by Richard I of England as a base for the Third Crusade, relations were difficult from the start, and in the Byzantine Empire actively hostile. The papal legate and the Latin Patriarch of Constantinople insisted first of all that the Pope must be commemorated in the diptychs, and then that other changes must be made in conformity with Western standards.[31] As a result commemoration of the Pope in the diptychs came to be a mark of collaboration with the invaders, indeed of treason. It also became a mark of submission to the local Latin authorities, political and ecclesiastical alike, to be deleted when any locality was liberated. In subsequent negotiations between the Greeks of the Empire of Nicaea and the papacy the heart of the difficulty was that a patriarch of Constantinople in communion with Rome, who consented to acknowledge the Pope as primate of the whole church, and to commemorate him in the diptychs, could not hope to recover possession of Saint Sophia, or authority over the Greeks in the Latin principalities.

The problem remained acute at the Second Council of Lyons in 1274 and at Ferrara and Florence in 1438–40. An understanding between Rome and Constantinople was and is difficult but not impossible. What was indeed impossible was the exercise of ecclesiastical authority by the Patriarch of Constantinople in the Latin principalities, for instance in the Venetian islands. But others had a like objection to the exercise of ecclesiastical authority by Rome, not only in the Byzantine Empire, but in Muslim lands and in central Asia.

The political pattern of Western Christendom as an entity where the Pope is over the kings no doubt goes back to ideals entertained by scholars in the eighth and ninth centuries, by the makers of the Donation of Constantine and the Pseudo-Isidorean decretals.[32] But it did not begin to be a practical political fact until the age of Hildebrand. The two Norman conquests of Sicily and England, the victory of the papacy in the investiture controversy and the First Crusade happened quickly one after another between 1066 and 1099. They must have impressed not only Byzantines like Anna Comnena[33] and Cinnamus[34] but Muslims and Jews with the idea that in the Latin West the Pope is emperor, a true Caliph.

This was the most formidable obstacle to papal diplomacy in dealing with the Mongols in the thirteenth century. The Popes evidently hoped to deal with these savage invaders of the civilized world as St Leo had dealt with Attila and his Huns, St Remigius with the pagan Franks, and other Christian missionaries with the Irish and the Anglo-Saxons. But in these cases the strength of the missionary's appeal lay in his physical weakness. He could speak of wisdom, but not of force. His threatenings of doom were in the world after death, not in the world of politics and armies. A more mixed approach had indeed been made to north German peoples after the victory of the Franks, and to some extent to the Scandinavians, although it is difficult to think of kings like St Olaf as bullied into conversion by military pressures. But overtures in the thirteenth century for an alliance with the Franks against the Muslim states to the south of the Mongol empire were bound to be read, as they inevitably were, in political terms.

It was this, I think, that both allured and alarmed the East Syrians and their Tartar and Turkish converts, called Nestorians by the friars, who took over the terminology of Chalcedonians and Jacobites in Syria and Palestine. On the one hand they were offered positions of responsibility and power by the Mongol khans. On the other they were deprived of what had been their greatest asset, if not the secret of their identity, that they could honestly say that we are in no way subjects of a foreign temporal power, Byzantine or Frankish. They feared the friars for this reason, but they had no sense of a spiritual or theological gulf between them and the Latins, who in many ways were much more like them, much more Dyophysite, than the Armenians or the Syrian Monophysites. They went to school with them. They wanted to learn from them, but they did not want to be identified with them. They were, however, when the Muslim element among the Turks and Tartars got the upper hand, and decided that all Christians are dangerous, especially Melkites, Maronites, Dyophysites, everyone who has to do with Western or Byzantine Catholics.

9

The Holy Places

In Jerusalem and Bethlehem Christian communions in schism with one another share the use of certain shrines, on conditions that have come to be incorporated in international agreements, of which the last and the most important, but not the first, was the Treaty of Paris after the Crimean War.[1] Rigidity in the *status quo*, as this condition of affairs has come to be called, has been modified in the last few years since common plans for the repair of the Holy Sepulchre have been worked out between the three main communities, Catholic, Orthodox and Armenian,[2] but it is still an obstacle to the development of closer relationships.

This is important for the general history of East and West because pilgrims of all nations have never ceased to encounter one another at Jerusalem, and to acquire impressions of one another in that particular and peculiar context. It is important to begin by emphasizing that the church of Jerusalem has been intercultural from the beginning. In the Acts of the Apostles there is tension between Hebrews and Hellenists (Acts 6.1). The Hellenists were Jews of the dispersion who came from a great variety of places and spoke a variety of languages at home, but spoke Greek with one another in preference to Hebrew which they did not understand, and Aramaic, which they did not use. So in the later history of the Church of Jerusalem Greek is the language of the pilgrims, including the many pilgrims whose pilgrimage ends at one of the churches and monasteries, but Palestinian Syriac is the language of the local orthodox people, who provide clergy and choirs for numerous parish churches, but do not often join the local monasteries. Those with monastic vocations go further afield, to St Catharine on Sinai or to monasteries in the Lebanon or in Syria.

Monastic choirs from early days might be multi-lingual. There were Latin and Greek monasteries, but also, for instance at St Sabbas, choirs with Greek, Syrian and Armenian divisions, who sang parts of the liturgy separately, but came together for the anaphora in Greek. St Sabbas at times had a Latin choir and this may be true of other monasteries. At Easter in the Holy Sepulchre, and at Pentecost in the church on Mount Sion, provision had to be made for a multitude of pilgrims, praising the Lord in their own languages, and similar problems arose at Christmas at Bethlehem.

That the Armenians had a recognized position in Jerusalem and at Bethlehem was no doubt one of the factors determining their reluctance to identify themselves completely with the Jacobite opposition to the Council of Chalcedon. This had little if any local support in Palestine. No doubt the local people were naturally inclined to an historical interpretation of scripture, in the sense of insisting that this or that happened here or there, and not elsewhere, and was not to be regarded as a text for mystical interpretation. They were ready to riot against Origenists in defence of Theodore of Mopsuestia, but accepted the Fifth Ecumenical Council where both were anathematized.[3] They had also non-theological reasons for remaining in communion with Constantinople and Rome as long as they could, while at the same time continuing to welcome Armenian pilgrims and some East Syrians from Mesopotamia. Those who keep hotels cannot afford to be isolationist.

After the Arab invasion however they were cut off from Byzantium, more completely for a time than from Rome. Patriarchs of Constantinople were not in their diptychs until 937.[4] The Pope continued to be an object of intercession, although after the death of Pope Benedict II in 685 they did not know his name.[5] There were still Greek choirs in Jerusalem, but many of those who sang in them had learnt Greek in order to sing. There were still Latin pilgrims and a Latin monastery. The presence of Armenians, Syrians, Georgians, is noted in pilgrim narratives.[6] All these belonged to the Orthodox church of the patriarchate, but no doubt Monophysite pilgrims appeared, Copts as well as Jacobites, and East Syrians were still received.

At the time of the Latin kingdom founded by the Crusaders the Armenians were still part of the church of Jerusalem. On the whole they found it easier to get on with the Latins than with the Greeks, and as we have seen this was also true of some of the Jacobites who came to Jerusalem at this time in greater numbers, and associated closely with the Armenians. The Copts appeared in strength in the period after the Latins lost Jerusalem, but while the Crusaders were still present in Palestine. The Sultan of Egypt was generally the master of Jerusalem from 1187 to 1291, although the Franks occupied it again for brief periods after 1229 and in 1241–3. The Sultan was naturally reluctant to admit Latin pilgrims or traders, and almost as reluctant to admit Greeks. But the Georgians at this time had a devout and powerful queen, who contributed to the repair of Golgotha, and acquired, by agreement with Saladin, some of the properties that the Latins had left there. The Georgians were Chalcedonians of unquestioned orthodoxy, but the Copts, who had, as always, friends in the Egyptian government, also moved in, bringing Ethiopian alms and pilgrims with them. The patriarchs of Jerusalem, who in this period of Egyptian rule were generally chosen by the local Orthodox notables, with the approval of the Sultan, and often came from the indigenous population, were hardly in a position to object to the presence of Copts and Ethiopians, as well as of Jacobites, who came in under Armenian protection. Their attitude to the Franciscans, when they came back about 1335 and rebuilt the Coenaculum on Mount Sion in 1340–2,[7] near the site of the old house church of Jerusalem, was probably ambivalent. The Franciscans were certainly Chalcedonians, like the Serbs who took over and restored the monastery of Saint Sabbas, south of Jerusalem, at about the same time.[8] Their presence would encourage pilgrims from lands in the possession of the Latins, like Cyprus, and from Western Europe. The local Christians needed the alms of pilgrims. On the other hand they were still smarting from the consequences of the Crusades which had brought them into suspicion and led to more and more harassment, with outbursts of actual persecution.

The patriarchs of Jerusalem were reluctant to endorse Byzantine lists of Latin errors and from time to time they made professions of allegiance to Rome and of assent to the decisions of the Second Council of Lyons in 1274. On the other hand they might also be expected to repudiate any idea that they were bound by papal policies. They were represented at Ferrara and Florence, but repudiated the result in 1443,[9] when a Crusade was said to be on the way.

The Ottoman Turks, who took over Jerusalem in 1516, were much more hostile to the West than the Sultans of Egypt had been. They were always engaged in war with the House of Austria. They turned the Franciscans out of the Coenaculum in 1523,[10] and probably intended to drive them out of the country altogether. But the patriarchs and the local Christians were their friends. As yet there was no schism in Jerusalem, although the community round the patriarchate were now more closely related to the Phanariot Greeks of the patriarchate of Constantinople, who clearly were in schism with Rome. In the years that followed two tendencies can be seen at work. On the one hand the Phanariots and a group of Armenians in the Turkish service in and around Constantinople, strove to extend their influence and authority in the Holy Places. An Armenian Patriarch of Constantinople was set up by the Turks and regarded by them as responsible for the good behaviour not only of Armenians in the Turkish empire, but of Copts and Jacobites, who formed a millet or subject community under his jurisdiction. This was naturally resented by the Coptic and Jacobite patriarchs, and by other Armenian patriarchs in other places, but these could not afford to fall out with the Constantinople Armenians.[11] The Phanariot Greeks around the patriarchate of Constantinople were generally more considerate of the authority of the patriarchs of Antioch, Alexandria and Jerusalem. But they wanted a decisive voice in their selection. The Patriarch of Alexandria, whose flock there was a small one, generally lived with the Phanariots in Constantinople. So did the Patriarch of Jerusalem from 1707[12] until the middle of the nineteenth century.

The other tendency that appears in the sixteenth and seventeenth centuries is for French diplomacy to foster opposition to the Phanariots and the Armenians of Constantinople. From 1535 France and Turkey were generally allies against Austria, and the French were able to encourage contacts with Western missionaries, not only among the Orthodox, but in Armenian and Jacobite circles. The Armenians had always been ambivalent in their attitude to Chalcedon, and had long been more hostile to the Greeks than to Rome. On the other hand it was very important to them to maintain their unity as a nation. They hoped to do this in communion with Rome, but those who felt closest to Catholic missionaries were unwilling to cut themselves off from the rest of the Armenian community. In September 1720, Peter Mauri reported that of 20,000 Armenians with Catholic sympathies in and around Constantinople, 5000 attended Catholic churches only, but 9000 might be seen at mass in a Catholic church and at an Armenian liturgy next Sunday, while 6000 kept their Catholic sympathies secret.[13]

Armenians had reason to be afraid of betraying their 'Frankish' sympathies by attending Latin churches in Constantinople. The use of the word Frank in controversy then and afterwards has often led to misunderstanding. It has no special reference to France, which at this time was anxious to distinguish herself from the Frankish image, and to encourage overtures.[14] The concessions that all Armenians would accept as opening moves, a declaration in 1727 by the two chief Armenian patriarchs of Constantinople and Ech-miadzin that denunciations of Chalcedon and the *Tome* were no longer in place and would be omitted from Armenian liturgical worship, was repeated in 1819–21 with some further explications by the Armenian Patriarch of Constantinople, Paul. It was acceptable to the French, who liked the idea of a national church in communion with Rome with its own standards, but not to Benedict XIII, who feared to encourage intercommunion between Catholic and schismatic Armenians in 1727, still less to the Vatican in 1820, after the collapse of Gallicanism in the French Revolution.[15]

The same reluctance to polarize between eirenical and hard line elements appears among the Melkites of Syria and Palestine. The schism in the patriarchate of Antioch developed through a disputed elected in 1724, in which the Latin missionaries were themselves divided between the candidates supported by Aleppo and Damascus. By Cyril VI, the Damascene candidate, though supported by the Wali of Damascus, failed to get the support of the Phanariots, and eventually in 1729–30, obtained recognition from Rome. His rival, Sylvester, elected at Aleppo, attached himself to the other patriarchs at the Phanar in Constantinople, who henceforth pursued a common line of antagonism to Latin missionaries.[16]

In the eighteenth century the Turkish Empire was vulnerable and more fearful of Western influence among its Christian subjects. In 1718 there was trouble over the repair of the Rotunda over the Holy Sepulchre, where the Greeks feared that the use of Catholic money, materials and craftsmen would strengthen Franciscan rights.[17] Soon after the Franciscans built churches of their own at Nazareth and Bethlehem, where they could celebrate the feasts in their own way and on their own days. The position had been made more difficult by the schism in the patriarchate of Antioch, and was further exacerbated by pronouncements from the Phanar on Latin ordinations and baptisms in 1755. These were not new. Where baptism was concerned they

renewed an old defence of baptism with the full ceremonie
where an Italian midwife had simply sprinkled the baby, bu
they were naturally read in the atmosphere of controversy a
meaning that the Greeks did not think Roman Catholic
Christians.[18] At this time the Phanariots were still collabor
ating with the Turks, but by the end of the century the Turk
were beginning to fear a Phanariot revolution supported by
Russia. In 1808–10 the Greeks were allowed to repair th
Holy Sepulchre after a fire, but after 1812, as the Greel
revolt became serious, many of them lost their jobs. The
Patriarch of Constantinople was hung in chains as respon
sible for the misdeeds of his millet, and for a time the Armen
ian share in the administration increased. The Patriarch Pau
was encouraged to proceed with his plan for union witl
Rome, which might win Turkey support from Catholi
Europe against Russia and the Greeks. But when the Papacy
would not play the Turks established a Catholic Armeniai
patriarch in 1831, with a millet including the Melkites, the
Catholic Syrians, and the Chaldeans united with Rome, a:
the millet of the older Armenian included the Jacobites anc
the Copts.[19] The Anglicans and the Prussians were encour
aged to set up a joint bishopric in Jerusalem,[20] and the Latir
Patriarch of Jerusalem to set up his seat there in 1847. A
about the same time the Greek Patriarch came from Con
stantinople to look after his rights on the spot, and more anc
more Jews returned.

Everyone was expecting the collapse of Turkey, including
the Turks, who sought to postpone it by fostering division:
between the peoples subject to them and the powers who
might have designs on their territory. Twice they succeeded
in the Crimean War of 1854–56 and in the Russo-Turkisl
war of 1876–78, in bringing in Western powers to protec
them against Russia. In this process the *status quo* was for
malized and fossilized to the advantage of the Brotherhooc
of the Holy Sepulchre, which had become entirely Greek, the
Custodes Terrae Sanctae, entirely Franciscan, the Armenians
the Copts, and some Muslim foundations and families. The

Ethiopians, who were there by leave of the Copts, the Jacobites, who depend on the Armenians, and the local Orthodox, who depend on the Greeks, were at a disadvantage. The Eastern Catholics had no place at all.

Russia after 1878 tried to help the Arabs in the patriarchates of Antioch and Jerusalem to shake themselves free from Phanariot dominance. At Damascus they succeeded in establishing an Arab Patriarchate of Antioch, still rather pro-Russian, with a large American emigration, especially in New York. At Jerusalem they came up against much stiffer resistance, which exacerbated differences between Arabs and Greeks after the collapse of the Orthodox Tsardom in 1917 and of the Turkish Empire in 1918. The British mandate maintained the *status quo* in Jerusalem as in Cyprus, where medieval churches are still mosques, and the division of Jerusalem between Israel and Jordan from 1948 to 1967 made change more difficult.

Two points need to be made about this long and complex story. The first is that the sharing of shrines, despite all the trouble that arises from it, reflects the continued harmony of Christians in the Holy Places before, in and after the age of the Crusades. The Armenians came in and stayed in as friends, and so did the Copts when their influence in Egypt was most valuable to the patriarchate, the Franciscans when Western pilgrims could come and were needed. The hardening of rights is due largely to Turkish and Phanariot fears, first of Austria, then of France and above all of Russia.

The second point is that while particular Catholic missionaries, Franciscans as well as Jesuits and Catholic Armenians, have always shown understanding of the need to maintain the identity and unity of particular Christian communities, Armenian, Melkite, Syrian, Chaldean, Rome, while anxious to preserve their rites, has always been chary of allowing those united with her to remain in communion with those who overtly repudiate her claims. This is very understandable, but it has produced sharp divisions between

103

Catholic and Gregorian Armenians, Catholic Melkites and Orthodox Arabs, who share common traditions.

It is sometimes suggested that the Franciscan rights in the Holy Places should be given to the Melkites who would then be the natural champions of the Arabs against the Greeks. But this might easily provoke conflict between Arab Orthodox and Arab Melkites, who are now much closer to each other than ever before. It would be better to wait for an Orthodox Patriarch of Jerusalem, a Greek or Syrian Christian, elected with the good will of the other Orthodox who would reduce but not extinguish Greek rights, and then arrange for some sort of parity between Greek and Latin rights within a community where Melkites and Orthodox are finding their way back into a united church. But Rome will now be wise enough not to insist on barring the gates of the shrines to pilgrims from Orthodox and Oriental, Monophysite churches not yet in union with Rome. Jerusalem has been, and could be again, a place where divisions between distinct traditions are healed, where the Arabs and the Latins are still together, and closer together as 'Arab Latins' liturgize in Arabic, where the Armenians have remained part of the Greek patriarchal church.

Now that the schism between the Orthodox and the Monophysites is on the way to being healed, both sides in this are more willing to recognize the possibility that the terms used by the others may be right, at any rate for them. This also applies to divisions between the Greek East and the Latin West. If the errors of the Latins are not after all heresy, the Roman primacy remains an authority for the Greeks,[21] the Syrian Jacobites and the Armenians, although they have not developed a clear positive doctrine of their own on the subject. I am not so sure about the Copts and the Ethiopians, who do seem to believe in a primacy of Alexandria at least equal to that of Rome. But I think that the Greeks and Russians, with help from the Armenians and from all kinds of Syrians, could help us to formulate some necessary distinctions between Rome's universal primacy and her patriarchal authority.[22] Her universal ordinary authority has been seen in terms of her metropolitan authority, like that of Alexandria, in the suburbican dioceses, extended first over the whole Western church in the eleventh and twelfth centuries, and then over the Eastern patriarchates in the twelfth and thirteenth. To restate this with the necessary distinctions is now both possible and needful, before we come to terms with controversies arising from the Reformation.

Appendix – Scholasticism

There are two ways of seeing scholasticism. In one it is the point at which Latin Christianity becomes fully articulate, with a theology and spirituality of its own which could and should be imposed not only on Latins, but on Irish and Poles, on Indians and Amerindians in Spanish America, and eventually on those hard nuts, the Germans, the Scandinavians and the Anglo-Saxons, finally on the hardest nuts of all, the Greeks, the Russians and the Copts, who believe that they have superior Christian cultures. This view of scholasticism, developed in the Catholic Reformation, was current in my youth in the form popularized by Hilaire Belloc, that 'the Faith is Europe and Europe is the Faith'. Europe here meant Latin Europe, almost as alien in England as in India. But scholasticism may also be considered, as we have seen it in these lectures, as a way of learning from non-Christian cultures, from Greek philosophers by way of the Jews and Arabs, who transmitted to the Latins what Syrian Christians had gathered from Babylonians, Greeks, Persians, Indians and Chinese. A return to this tradition in scholastic enquiry led Dominicans to learn from modern psychology, Jesuits like Teilhard de Chardin from the scientific study of primitive man. It has led to enquiries into Hinduism and Buddhism, and into forms of Christian experience, not only on Mount Athos and elsewhere in the Christian East, but in the North and West, where Catholics learn from Protestants and Pentecostalists.

Catholics and Protestants alike are naturally and rightly

interested in the historical study of primitive Christianity and of the history behind the Old and New Testaments. Protestants have pioneered in this, since the original motive of the Protestant Reformation was the discovery of authentic early Christianity. But Catholic interest in the past history of the human race and of the church is more comprehensive, less limited to the recovery of the original meaning of biblical themes, where Catholic expectations may be more modest than Protestant ones, because these themes have had changing meanings through the whole course of church history, and none of these meanings are folly. We should therefore be open to learn from present as well as from past experience, from heresies that are still alive and from other religions as well as from conflicts in the past.

I became a Catholic myself through listening with Catholics to Buddhism and Pentecostalism in the same times and places. But I was also aware of Catholics who saw in the renewal of Orthodoxy, not only in Russia and Romania but in the Russian emigration and in the Middle East, something that is happening to the church, and not altogether outside it. Catholics can learn from Hindus and Buddhists as well as from Pentecostalists. They have learnt a great deal from Lutherans, Calvinists and Anglicans, as well as from the Orthodox, but there is a real difference between schisms in the East, including the Monophysite and Nestorian schisms, and those that happened at the Reformation. The Eastern schisms happened gradually, through a series of misunderstandings about terms, and they will be healed gradually, as Rome comes to understand that she cannot impose her kind of Latin scholasticism as the only standard whereby orthodoxy can be judged. This involves a new look at theological differences between East and West, as well as at those approaches to the incarnation that used to be called Antiochene and Alexandrian, but might better be called Babylonian and Egyptian, or East and West Syrian. These geographical terms are not very appropriate, since Monophysite approaches are found in Mesopotamia, and Eastern approaches to the doctrine of the Trinity in Western theology, Catholic as well as Anglican. As all traditional Christians believe that Christ is perfect God and perfect man, so East and West confess together that the Spirit proceeds from the Father and the Son. But the East would distinguish between his temporal mission, his procession of manifestation, and the more mysterious procession of his being, of which all that can be said is that it is from the Father.[1]

For Further Reading

A. S. Atiyah, *History of Eastern Christianity*, London and Notre Dame 1968 (by a Copt).

L. W. Brown, *Indian Christians of St Thomas*, Cambridge 1956.

Cambridge Medieval History, Vol IV, *The Eastern Roman Empire*, 1936, *The Byzantine Empire*, in two parts 1966–7.

C. Couasnon, *The Church of the Holy Sepulchre*, London 1974.

C. Dawson, *The Mongol Mission*, narratives of the Friars, New York 1955.

H. F. T. Duckworth, *The Church of the Holy Sepulchre*, London 1922.

The Eastern Churches and Catholic Unity, ed., Maximus IV Sayegh, London and Edinburgh 1963.

L'Eglise et les Eglises, études et Travaux offerts a Dom Lambert Beauduin, Chevetogne, Belgium 1954.

D. J. Geanakoplos, *Byzantine East and Latin West*, New York and Evanston 1966.

E. R. Hardy, *Christian Egypt*, Oxford and New York 1952.

D. Mathew, *Ethiopia*, London 1947.

Gervase Mathew, *Byzantine Aesthetics*, London 1963.

O. Meinardus, *Christian Egypt, Ancient and Modern*, Cairo 1965.

J. Meyendorff, *The Orthodox Church*, London and New York 1964.

D. Obolensky, *The Byzantine Commonwealth*, London 1971.

J. Pelikan, *The Spirit of Eastern Christendom*, London and Chicago 1974.

H. F. D. Prescott, *Jerusalem Journey*, London 1954.

S. Runciman, *The Eastern Schism*, Oxford 1955.

S. Runciman, *History of the Crusades*, in 2 vols, 1951–4.

A. Schmemann, *The Historical Road of Eastern Orthodoxy*, London 1963.

P. Sherrard, *The Greek East and the Latin West*, Oxford 1959.

E. Tisserant, *Eastern Christianity in India*, Maryland 1957.

K. T. Ware, *The Orthodox Church*, London and New York 1962.

W. A. Wigram, *The Separation of the Monophysites*, London 1923.

Abbreviations

ACW	*Ancient Christian Writers*, London and Westminster (Maryland) 1946.
BO	*Bibliotheca Orientalis*, ed. J. S. Assemanus, Rome 1719–28.
Byz. Pat.	*The Byzantine Patriarchate* by George Every, 2nd ed., London 1962.
ByZ	*Byzantinische Zeitschrift*, Leipzig 1892.
CAH	*Cambridge Ancient History*, Cambridge 1923–39, 1970.
CSHB	*Corpus Scriptorum Historiae Byzantinae*, Bonn 1826–97.
CSCO	*Corpus Scriptorum Christianorum Orientalium*, Paris-Louvain 1903.
DNB	*Dictionary of National Biography*, London 1885–1900.
DThC	*Dictionnaire de Théologie Catholique*, Paris 1899–1950.
Eccles. Hist.	*Ecclesiastical History* (of Eusebius, Sozomen, Evagrius etc.)
ECQ	*Eastern Churches Quarterly*, Ramsgate and London 1936–64.
ECR	*Eastern Churches Review*, Oxford 1966–78.
ERE	*Encyclopaedia of Religion and Ethics*, Edinburgh 1908–21.
Fliche-Martin	*Histoire de l'Eglise*, ed. A. Fliche and V. Martin, Paris 1935–60.

Hist. Anc.	*Histoire ancien de l'Eglise,* by L. Duchesne, Paris 1911–2.
H-L.	Conciliengeschichte by C. J. Hefele, French ed. by H. Leclerq, Paris 1907–14.
Liber	*Book.*
Mansi	Concilia Sacrorum Conciliorum amplissima Collectio, ed. J. D. Mansi, Florence and Venice 1758–98, reprinted Paris 1901–12.
MPG	Patrologia Graeco-Latina, ed. J. P. Migne, Paris 1857–64.
MPL	Patrologia Latina, Paris 1844–55.
PO	Patrologia Orientalis, Paris 1907.
VIème Siécle	*L'Eglise au Sixième Siécle,* by L. Duchesne, Paris 1925.
SC	*Sources chrétiennes,* Paris 1941ff.

Notes

1 Eastern-Christianity Yesterday and Today

1. See Nicholas Zernov, *The Russian Religious Renaissance of the Twentieth Century*, London and New York 1963.

2. This happened at the Council of the Russian Church that took place during the Revolution and continued into 1918.

3. In the Patriarchate of Antioch an Arab, Meletios, was elected with Russian support to Damascus in 1899. Constantinople and the Turkish government refused to recognize him but eventually accepted his successor.

4. They objected to the presence of Mikhail Rodzianko, who was president of the Duma at the time of the Tsar's abdication, at a synod at Karlovtsi in Yugoslavia in December 1921. See N. Zernov's notes from his diary on this in *ECR* VII, 2 (1975), pp. 167–8.

5. See D. A. Lowrie, *Saint Sergius in Paris*, London 1954, and A. Kniazeff, *L'Institut Saint Serge*, Paris 1974.

6. See an article by A. Kazen-Bek published in Russian in Moscow in 1969, translated into French in *Istina*, Paris 1971, p. 107.

7. See Kniazeff, op. cit., pp. 40f., on Mott's raising money for Saint-Serge.

8. See S. Runciman, *The Eastern Schism*, Oxford 1955, drawing on F. Dvornik, *The Photian Schism*, Cambridge 1948, and my own *Byzantine Patriarchate*.

9. See J. Meyendorff and others, *The Primacy of Peter in the Orthodox Church*, London and New York 1963, second edition, New York 1973, ET from French of Paris 1960.

10. See *Byz. Pat.*, p. 187, citing Balsamon in MPG 138, col. 967–8, and Demetrius Chomatenus in MPG 119, col. 957–60, both writing *c.* 1200.

11. See *The Eastern Churches and Catholic Unity*, ed., Maximus IV Sayegh (Melkite Patriarch of Antioch), London and Edinburgh 1963.

12. See J. L. Heby, *The Russian Church and the World Council of Churches*, Belfast 1978.

13. See Peter Chirico, *Infallibility*, London and New York 1977.

113

14. Grotto-ferrara, which still survives, was founded by St Neilos in 1002–4.

2 Merchants, Monks and Missionaries

1. In Africanus, as preserved by George Syncellus in *CSHB* (ed. Dindorf), Bonn 1820, pp. 187–8; in MPG 10, col. 69; and in Martin Routh, *Reliquiae Sacrae* ii, Oxford 1846, p. 265, Abraham goes down into Egypt in a time of famine, as Jacob does, and returns enriched by the profits of trade. He bought in Egypt and sold in Palestine.

2. MPG 88, col. 73A, ET by J. W. McCrindle in Hakluyt Society ed., Cambridge 1897, p. 24; French by W. Wolska-Comus in *SC*, Paris 1968, p. 306. McCrindle understands this as referring to a different Abraham.

3. See D. B. Quinn in *Geographical Journal*, September 1961, pp. 277–85, 'The argument for the English discovery of America between 1480 and 1494'; J. A. Williamson, *The Cabot Voyage and Bristol Discovery*, Hakluyt Society II, no. CXX, Cambridge 1962.

4. Pliny, *Natural History*, VI, 84–9.

5. David Meredith in *Journal of Roman Studies*, XLIII (1953), pp. 38–40, reports inscriptions in Latin and Greek on the road from Coptos to Berenice, with the signature of Lysas of (slave or freedom of) Annius Plocamus, with dates corresponding to July AD 6. He argues that Plocamus was already in control of the customs there and remained until the reign of Claudius, since the embassy brought back from Ceylon appeared in his reign, but Pliny may have made a mistake about the date.

6. *Natural History*, VI, 100–101.

7. See Mortimer Wheeler, *Rome Beyond the Imperial Frontiers*, Pelican edition, London 1955, p. 56.

8. See J. Innes Miller, *The Spice Trade of the Roman Empire*, Oxford 1969, pp. 20–26.

9. Ibid., pp. 90–1.

10. Ibid., pp. 123, 127–31.

11. See A. H. M. Jones, in *Roman Economy*, ed., P. Brunt, Oxford 1974, pp. 146–9.

12. See M. Carey and E. H. Warmington, *Ancient Explorers*, 1929, Pelican edition, London 1963, pp. 195–7, Miller, *The Spice Trade,* pp. 127–31. The source is an account by the Macedonian merchant Maes of his journey to 'the stone tower' where he met the Chinese, incorporated by Marinus in his geographical work of the early second century AD, and so in the geography of Ptolemy.

13. Tung Fu in an article in *ERE*, XII (1921), p. 76, shows reason to think that the 28 lunar mansions in the ecliptic are of Chinese origin and reached Babylonia later through India.

14. What purported to be a careful copy of this inscription was sent

through the post to a museum in Brazil in 1872. The few who had an opportunity to examine it came to the conclusion that it must be forged, but Cyrus H. Gordon comes to a different conclusion in *Riddle in History*, London and New York 1974. To him I owe my reference to Jews in a Phoenician fleet in the History of Herodotus 7.89.

15. See Josephus, *Antiquities*, Book XX, chs 2 and 3, with comment in the article on Adiabene in the *Jewish Encyclopedia* II, Jerusalem 1971.

16. The Falashas in Ethiopia are 'black Jews' who know neither Midrash nor Talmud, and probably became proselytes before these collections took shape in the second century AD.

17. Profession to the religious life still takes place at Mass. In the early church the Paschal Liturgy was the great occasion for baptisms and other celebrations, and a most appropriate time for vows of celibacy, but also no doubt for the exchange of marriage vows.

18. See *Acts of Thomas*, ed., A. F. J. Klijn, Leyden 1962, pp. 27ff., and for a more general treatment of the history of the community L. W. Brown, *The Indian Christians of St Thomas*, Cambridge 1956.

19. See A. H. M. Jones, *Roman Economy*, p. 149. John of Ephesus in his *Lives of the Eastern Saints*, XXXI, in PO, XVIII, trans E. W. Brooks, pp. 576–85, tells of two brothers, Elijah and Theodore, who worked for a merchant for twenty years with salaries increasing from 10 to 30 solidi, and then went into business on their own at a hospice run by Elijah's wife, where Monophysite monks were entertained.

20. Procopius, *Gothic War*, IV, 17.

21. In his *Bibliotheca*, MPG 103, col. 138; from Theophanes, not the Byzantine historian of the eighth century, but another earlier writer.

22. See articles in the *DNB* on the brothers Thomas and John Lombe, who claimed to have discovered the secrets of mechanical silk-spinning by espionage in Genoa, although it was alleged that all their information was in a book published in Padua in 1607. It is clear however that their mill at Derby was in operation by 1727 and stimulated the mechanization of the textile industry as a whole.

23. MPG 88, col. 96–7, ET by McCrindle, pp. 47–51, Wolska-Conus, pp. 352–3.

24. See H. Hess, *Canons of the Council of Sardica*, Oxford 1958, pp. 83–5, on canons 19 of Elvira and 11–12 of Sardica.

25. Gregory the Great, *Epistle* 26 in Lib. XIII, MPL 77, col. 1278; see F. Holmes Dudden, *St Gregory the Great*, London 1905, vol. I, p. 382. The Bishop, Paschasius of Naples, had lost a good deal of money on voyages.

26. See J. Labourt, *Le Christianisme dans l'empire Perse*, Paris 1904, pp. 148–50.

27. See Thomas of Marga, *The Book of the Governors*, trans E. A. W.

Budge, London 1893, p. 94.

28. See J. Foster, *The Church of the Tang Dynasty*, London 1939, for the monument discovered at Sianfu in 1625 by a Jesuit missionary. This refers with approval to Christians in the Roman Empire, and the Syrian Christians in Kerala at first received the Portuguese with enthusiasm as friends. The same seems often to have been true of friars who travelled among Nestorian converts in Central Asia in the Middle Ages.

3 From Alexandria into Egypt

1. A. H. M. Jones, *Cities of the Eastern Roman Provinces*, Oxford 1937, pp. 328–9.

2. The late W. C. Hayes in *CAH*, third edition, I, 1, Cambridge 1970, pp. 173–4, rejects 4241 as a date for the first dynasty, opting for something like 3100 BC. This would still give 2600 years of Egyptian history before the Persian empire.

3. Jones, op. cit., pp. 329ff.

4. MPG 111, col. 982 in Latin translated from Arabic by the English scholar, Edward Pocock.

5. The same name for the first patriarch is in Eusebius, *Eccles. Hist.* 2, c.24.1. Other material in Eutychius resembles citations from Julius Africanus in Syncellus and elsewhere.

6. One of a series of letters of Dionysius cited in Eusebius, *Eccles. Hist.* 6.c.40; 7.c.11. They may not all be in the right order, but they are original, and probably taken from a collection of letters to his people, confused before it reached Eusebius.

7. Ascribed to St Athanasius in MPG 26, col. 835–78, ET by E. A. W. Budge in *Paradise of the Fathers*, London 1907, vol. 1, pp. 3–75.

8. The word used in MPG 26, col. 844A, becomes the regular word for a nunnery. It is used quite naturally, and I think we may assume that 'the virgins' house' was well known in many churches before there were any men's communities.

9. MPG 26. col. 857A.

10. See W. H. Frend, *The Donatist Church*, Oxford 1952 and 1971. The Donatists, like the Meletians, had martyrs whom the churches would not recognize, presumably those involved in brawls with the police in Numidia and in the back streets of Carthage, as in upper Egypt and the back streets of Alexandria.

11. See H-L. I, 1, pp. 388–403 on the Meletian question at Nicaea.

12. In canon 4; no exception to this was made when the special positions of Rome and Alexandria were recognized in canon 6. Bishops must consecrate bishops.

13. See H. I. Bell, *Jews and Christians in Egypt*, British Museum, London 1924, pp. 45–71, especially pp. 57–62. He cites a Meletian letter

saying that 'Athanasius was very despondent when he heard of the arrest of Archelaus,' and comments 'it is hardly conceivable that the confederates can have acted without at least his tacit consent. We must conclude that there was a germ of truth in the picture given of Athanasius by his enemies as a self-willed, unruly man, apt to treat even the imperial authority with contempt'.

14. Here St Athanasius himself tells the story in chapter 87 of his *Apology* in MPG 25, col. 405A. He cites witnesses who were present when his adversaries said 'Athanasius has tried to prevent the corn being sent from Alexandria to your country.' But when he goes on to say that 'the wrath of the Emperor proved it, for he who had written letters to condemn their iniquitous dealings, flared up on hearing this calumny, and sent us to Gaul without waiting for our defence,' he implies that something has gone seriously wrong. He does not even say what defence he would have made, but I have presumed in the text that he would have disavowed any responsibility for the consequences of comments on the politics of the court to workers in the docks.

15. In canon 6.

16. See Derwas J. Chitty, *The Desert a City*, Oxford 1966, pp. 7–45.

17. There are many references to Meletian communities and some that may be to Athanasian, in Bell, op. cit., pp. 37–99.

18. Sozomen, *Eccles. Hist.* III, c.20, in MPG 67, col. 1099C.

19. See the article on Liberius in *DThC* IX, c.638. In his *History of the Arians for the Monks* in MPG 25, c.741–3, St Athanasius seems to distinguish clearly between Liberius, who consented to condemn him, but refused to compromise himself with a formulary, and Hosius, who accepted a confused formulary, but would not condemn his friend. This is in character with both parties. Hosius was very old by 357 and had grown up before ideas were clarified in controversy. Liberius as Pope had to be careful about committing Rome to anything unsatisfactory, but he would also be aware of problems of order in a big city, and impressed by the evidence of association between St Athanasius and the criminal classes provided by his continued success in escaping arrest.

20. Jerome, *Against the Luciferians*, 19, in MPL 23, col. 172C.

4 *The Kingship of Christ in Egypt and Babylon*

1. Philo of Alexandria was the great Jewish master of allegorical interpretation of the Old Testament. Little is known of his life, except that he was a leading member of the Alexandrian Jewish community in AD 40. He probably died soon after. His works must have had a considerable circulation in the synagogues of the dispersion while Christianity was spreading in them, and they survived in Christian hands.

2. See R. P. C. Hanson, *Allegory and Event*, London 1959, for modern

criticism of these, and for more sympathetic treatment Danielou on *Origen*, Paris 1948, London 1955, and Pere Henri de Lubac, *Histoire et Esprit*, Paris 1950, and *Exégèse Mediévale*, vol. 1, Paris 1959. See also Jo Tigcheler, *Didyme l'Aveugle et l'exégèse allégorique*, Nijmegen, Holland 1977,

3. An Egyptian account of this is in *Coptic Apocryphal Gospels* ed., Forbes Robinson, Cambridge 1896, where 'an image of alabaster called Elachistes' falls with others around it, before Mary, who 'sat on the judgment seat. Thunders sounded, lightnings flashed, and the dead arose and came out of their tombs.' Other accounts are in the Latin *Pseudo-Matthew*, c. xxii–iv, and the Arabic *Gospel of the Infancy* x.

4. Described by Henri Frankfort in *Kingship and the Gods*, Chicago 1948, pp. 70–77, 97–8.

5. *CAH*, I II, third edition 1970, p. 195.

6. The story told by Robin Lane Fox in *Alexander*, London 1973, pp. 290ff.

7. Here Plotinus and the Christians, including Origen, agree against the Gnostics. See A. H. Armstrong, *Introduction to Ancient Philosophy*, fourth edition, London 1965, pp. 173–4, 193–4.

8. Philo's influence is difficult to determine but Numenius, whose influence was considerable, certainly interpreted the Old Testament Platonically. See John Dillon, *The Middle Platonists*, London 1977, p. 378.

9. See Frankfort, op. cit., pp. 299–301 on Babylonian sons of the gods.

10. See R. R. Bolgar, *The Classical Heritage*, Cambridge 1954, pp. 79–80.

11. I would ascribe the *Didache*, 'the teaching of the Apostles', to such a church, but J. P. Audet would put it very early and at Antioch itself in his edition, Paris 1958.

12. See R. H. Connolly's introduction to his edition of the *Didascalia of the Apostles*, Oxford 1929, pp. LVII–LXVIII.

13. For like problems at Jerusalem see *The Pilgrimage of Etheria*, ed., M. L. McClure and C. L. Feltoe, London 1919, p. 94.

14. Their correspondence is in MPG 11, col. 41–86.

15. Eusebius, *Eccles. Hist.*, 7, c.27–30.

16. Ibid., c.30.

17. There is no doubt that one of the Councils on the case of Paul of Samosata condemned the use of the word, but accounts of this reflect attempts to explain it away after the Council of Nicaea in 325, when it became the orthodox term for explaining not only relations between the persons of the Trinity, but the identity of Christ's humanity with their own. Marcellus and Eustathius of Antioch, who were prominent on this occasion, were both suspected of some sympathy with Paul, whose surviving followers were reconciled at this time to the great church of Antioch

118

by Eustathius. The term had also been used by Origen and Dionysius of Rome, and its Latin equivalent, *consubstantialis*, was used in the West in the Nicene sense. I think that Paul used it, as St Hilary thought, to affirm the identity of the Word of God in Christ with God himself. No doubt the word was used in common discourse as meaning 'of one stuff', but I find it hard to believe that anyone was ever suspected of believing that the Father and Son were 'made of the same materials'. See G. L. Prestige, *God In Patristic Thought*, London 1952, pp. 202–9, where St Athanasius is preferred to St Hilary, and full references are given.

18. As Maurice Wiles supposed in *The Making of Christian Doctrine*, Cambridge 1957, pp. 56–7.

19. Theodoret, *Eccles. Hist.*, I, c.3.

20. See canon 19, H-L I I, pp. 615–18.

21. So St Athanasius in his *History of the Arians*, MPG 25, col. 697. This has been explained by Helena's devotion to Lucian the martyr and his disciples, but it may have more to do with her activities in the holy places. Eustathius no doubt had views on the identity of sites which her methods of directing excavation did not confirm.

22. See R. V. Sellers, *Eustathius of Antioch*, Cambridge 1928.

23. Paulinus, the bishop of the Eustathian 'little church', was ordained in a most irregular way by Lucifer of Cagliari, who later went into schism, in 362. Rome continued to recognize him as the Bishop of Antioch until he died in 388. His rival, Melitius, was generally recognized as orthodox in the East by 379, when they agreed what whoever died first the other should succeed him. Contrary to expectation, Paulinus was the survivor, and the larger church would not take him. Rome objected to this, and did not recognize Flavian even after Paulinus died, but she did nothing to encourage the continuation of the schism. See L. Duchesne, *Hist. Anc.*, II, Paris 1911, pp. 606–11, J. R. Palanque in Fliche-Martin III, Paris 1936, p. 450.

5 The Monophysite Question

1. See J. Danielou, *Origen*, London 1955, pp. 133–8 on his critical work on the text of the Old Testament.

2. See Eusebius, *Eccles. Hist.* 7, c.24–5 for Bishop Nepos of Arsinoe, who expected the second coming in the middle of the third century.

3. St Cyril's critics were right in thinking that his key phrase, 'One is the nature of the Word made flesh', taken as he thought from a letter of St Athanasius, was not his, but more probably the work of Apollinaris, one of a number of 'Apollinarian forgeries', circulated by his friends after his condemnation under other names.

4. When Pope Zosimus came down on the side of St Augustine against Pelagius in 418, Julian of Eclanum and other bishops took refuge in the

East, where they worked to reverse this verdict and to have St Augustine condemned as a heretic. Marius Mercator acted as St Augustine's agent in the conduct of controversy against them between 420–30.

5. The letters are in F. Loofs, *Nestoriana*, Halle 1905, pp. 165–8, 170–2.

6. Cassian's *Seven Books on the Incarnation* in MPL 50 reflect his recent encounter with Leporius of Treves, condemned at Marseilles, but later persuaded by St Augustine to change his views, which resembled those of Marcellus of Ancyra.

7. In St Cyril's twelfth anathema he insisted that 'The Word of God suffered in the flesh, and tasted death in the flesh, and was made the first born from the dead, as He is life and life-giving, as God'. To him this was the implication of 'God was born', of *Theotokos*. But such language was not only unacceptable in the Mesopotamian tradition, but offensive to some pious ears in Rome.

8. So L. Duchesne argued in *Hist. Anc.* III, pp. 372–3.

9. This was the central point of the agreement between St Cyril and John of Antioch, prepared by Theodoret, in 433, that 'There has been a union of two natures.'

10. The report of the trial in Mansi, *Concilia* VI, col. 744–8.

11. The famous *Tome* in MPL 54, col. 755–82 as *Epistle* 28, and in many collections of documents relating to the history of the church.

12. Michael the Syrian's chronicle was edited with a French translation by J. B. Chabot, Paris 1899–1910. The passage in vol. II, 1901, p. 29, is most probably from John of Ephesus, whose history is certainly used by Michael in other places. I see no reason why he in the sixth century, or Michael in the twelfth, should have invented this explanation, which makes Dioscorus more foolish, if less brutal, than he appears to be in the orthodox tradition. If he was so foolish as to take Eutyches seriously, he may have thought that the *Tome* was written on an off day.

13. This appears from his *Epistles* 69–71 in MPL 54, col. 890–96.

14. This was the result of trouble at the fourth session on 17 October, when the Egyptian bishops, prepared to condemn Eutyches, could not square St Leo with St Cyril. See Mansi, *Concilia* VII, col. 49–61.

15. Ibid., col. 116 (22 October).

16. See his helpful words in *Epistle* 165, MPL 54, col. 1155–90: 'Although in the one Lord Jesus Christ, the true Son of God and of man, the person of the Word and flesh is one, who without separation or division takes actions common to both of them, nevertheless we must discern the qualities of these actions, and discern . . . where it is that the majesty of the divinity is lowered; what it is that the flesh without the Word does not do, and what it is that the Word without the flesh does not effect . . . Without the power of the Word the Virgin would not conceive or bear, and without the true reality of the flesh his infancy

would not have lain in swaddling bands.'

17. Mansi, *Concilia* VI, col. 1097. It is clear that this happened, but when is not so certain, perhaps at Nicaea before the Council was moved to Chalcedon. Dioscorus may have tried to begin, like Theophilus and St Cyril in similar circumstances, before others arrived.

18. E.g., the *Henoticon* of 482 in Evagrius, *Eccles. Hist.* 3, c.14, and the so-called 'second Henoticon', ibid., 5 c.4. Both are translated in W. H. Frend, *The Rise of the Monophysite Movement*, Cambridge 1972, with other documents bearing on negotiations.

19. Of these the most persistent were the *Acoimetoi*, the 'sleepless monks' in Constantinople, who persisted in opposition to St Cyril's anathemas after Rome approved them.

20. L. Duchesne in *L'Eglise au sixième siécle,* Paris 1925, p. 59 and note, shows that in the letters of St Leo's successors from Hilary to Hormisdas (461–523) 'St Cyril is not mentioned, except as presiding over the Council of Ephesus.'

21. Among these were Pope Anastasius II (496–8), and Dionysius Exiguus, a Scythian monk who translated St Cyril's twelve anathemas into Latin. See Duchesne in *VIème Siécle*, pp. 14–15, 112–14, 134–8, and my own *Byz. Pat.*, London 1962, pp. 36–8 and refs.

22. MPL 66, col. 20–24.

23. An interesting consequence of this controversy is a sermon in *Coptic Apocryphal Gospels* on the death of the Blessed Virgin, in which her body dissolves and corrupts according to nature,' but becomes 'altogether incorruptible and indissoluble to ages of ages'. when Our Lord appears on the chariot of the cherubim, the soul of the Virgin wrapt in his bosom,' and her soul and body are reunited after 206 days, sufficient time for a proper dissolution. This sermon is ascribed to Theodosius of Alexandria in the year of his death, 567. He was therefore excluded by Fr Martin Jugie from the list of those who believe in the Assumption of the Blessed Virgin, but before this was defined in terms that leave open the relation of her resurrection to our own. In the Theodosian view it anticipates ours.

24. See R. Draguet, *Julian d'Halicarnasse et sa controverse avec Sevère d'Antioche sur l'incorruptibilité du corps de Christ*, Louvain 1924, and texts of Severus edited by Robert Hespel in CSCO 104 and 126, Louvain 964–69.

25. *Breviarium* XXII in MPL 68, col. 1041; also in Victor Tununensis, *Chronicon*, sub. 543, MPL 68, col. 957. See Facundus in MPL 67, col. 861. Duchesne in *VIème siécle*, pp. 177–8 and my article on Vigilius and Justinian in *Heythrop Journal* XX, 3, London 1979, pp. 259ff.

26. See A. Guillaumont, *Les 'Kephalaia Gnostica' d'Evagre le Pontique et l'histoire d'Origenisme chez les Grecs et les Syriens*, Paris 1962, following his edition of Evagrius in PO 28, fasc. 1, from the Syriac version,

published 1958.

27. The first text survives only in fragments. The revised edict is in MPG 86a, col. 993–1036.

28. See especially the anathemas in col. 1013–18, followed at the Fifth Ecumenical Council in 553.

29. A number of statements may be found in his works in MPL 69. His final *Constitutum* in col. 67–114 has been much admired. This was made during the Ecumenical Council, but withdrawn when the Pope finally decided to acquiesce in the Council's not very different decisions.

30. The profession of faith made by Pope Pelagius at this time may be found in A. Hahn, *Bibliothek der Symbol*, Breslau 1897, pp. 334–6. F. Dvornik in *The Photian Schism*, Cambridge 1948, pp. 435–7, shows that it continued to be made by Popes at their coronation until Gregory VI dropped the custom, as sensitive to the implications of any idea that the Pope could be judged by the Emperor or by the other patriarchs.

31. See J. Labourt, *Christianisme dans l'Empire Perse*, Paris 1904, pp. 277–80.

32. See *Byz. Pat.*, p. 51, citing MPL 69, col. 400.

6 *The Dyothelite Controversy*

1. See my own article on 'The Monophysite question, ancient and modern' in *ECR* III, 4, Oxford 1971, pp. 405–6 and refs. Much of the modern impetus to reconciliation between Orthodox and Monophysite Eastern Churches involved in the ecumenical movement has come from South India, where the Malankara Monophysites have an East Syrian and a Catholic background, and from Ethiopia. It seems to be clear that the Copts no longer regard Chalcedon as interpreted by Catholic tradition in the Fifth and Sixth Councils as Nestorian.

2. F. Dvornik in *National Churches and the Church Universal*, London 1944, pp. 13–15, has shown that Greeks and Syrians had their own churches and even bishops in Armenia before there was any schism, but the Armenians did not have bishops outside Armenia until much later and long continued to be associated with the Orthodox community in Jerusalem. Some in Armenia itself held Chalcedonian views and were not excommunicated.

3. The contemporary life of Maximus in MPG 90 at col. 976 ascribes the Monothelite formulary to Athanasius, no doubt to avoid blaming Pope Honorius. There is other evidence in a sermon on Anastasius, a monk of St Sabbas near Jerusalem, in MPG 89, col. 1844, that he was expected to be recognized by the government as Patriarch of Antioch. See W. H. Frend, *The Rise of the Monophysite Movement*, Cambridge 1972, p. 347.

4. Fr Polycarp Sherwood, introducing Maximus in *ACW* XXI, 1955, p. 7, says 'about the year 613–14'. He had a disciple by 618.

5. Patricia Crone and Michael Cook, *Hagarism*, Cambridge 1977, pp. 3–9, citing *Doctrine Jacobi baptizati*, ed., N. Bonwetsch, Berlin 1910, pp. 86f. Confirmation is claimed on p. 152 from the *Continuatio Byzantia Arabica* in *Monumenta Germaniae Historica, Aust. Ant.* XI, pp. 336–8, which puts the death of Mahomet and the succession of Abubeccar after the fall of Damascus, but this was assembled in Spain a century later.

6. *Histoire d'Heraclius by Sepeos, Bishop of the Pakradouni* (so in BM) trans., F. Macler, Paris 1904, pp. 94–6. For the date see *Hagarism*, p. 157.

7. *Hagarism*, pp. 7, 158.

8. *Hagarism*, p. 158, note 41 and refs to Muhammad ibn Ishaq, *Life of Muhammad*.

9. This shift in orientation is the heart of the argument of *Hagarism* and will no doubt be assailed by orthodox Muslims and Islamists, but it is difficult for them to deny that the original direction of Muslim prayer was to Jerusalem.

10. MPG 91, col. 540–42. See P. Sherwood, *An annotated date-list of the works of Maximus Confessor, Studia Anselmica* XXX, Rome 1952, pp. 40f.

11. See John Meyendorff, *Christ in Eastern Christian Thought*, second edition, Crestwood, New Jersey 1975, pp. 131–51.

12. See Meyendorff, *Byzantine Theology*, New York 1974, p. 38.

13. MPG 91, col. 77–80.

14. Ibid., col. 308–9.

15. MPG 90, col. 889.

16. Infra, p. 82.

17. *Epistle 30* in *Liber Epistularum*, ed., Rubens Duval, CSCO 1905, p. 154.

18. This complicated question is considered by Fr Sherwood in his introduction to the *ACW* volume, pp. 14–20.

19. So it appears in Duchesne, *VIème siécle*, p. 409.

20. Ibid., p. 407.

21. Ibid., pp. 451–3, 458–61.

22. Ibid., pp. 461–6.

23. Mansi, *Concilia* XI, col. 637–40.

24. MPG 90, col. 891.

25. Theophanes in *CSHB*, Bonn 1839, p. 507, MPG 108, col. 680.

26. See especially Lars Thunberg, *Microcosm and Mediator, the Theological Anthropology of Maximus Confessor*, Lund, Sweden, 1965.

7 Christians under Muslim Rule

1. Maronite scholars have argued that their difference with the Melkites arose from continued resistance, and not from Monothelitism. So did Abraham Ecchelensis in a letter of 13 July 1654 to Jean Morin, printed

in a collection of letters, *Antiquitates ecclesiae orientalis*, ed., Richard Simon and published in London in 1682, pp. 449–70. A modern view is given by Philip Hitti, *Lebanon in History*, London 1957, pp. 249, 448–9, 521–2. Justinian II certainly disavowed the Mardaites to get a truce in 694. The Maronite centres were in territory controlled by the resistance.

2. See P. Hitti, *History of Syria*, second edition, London 1957, p. 414, for the terms of the capitulation in which the Bishop of Damascus and Mansur-ibn-Sanjun were both involved.

3. See H. Marrou, *A Short History of Education in Antiquity*, ET, London 1956.

4. See W. Wright, *Short History of Syriac Literature*, London 1895, pp. 64–5.

5. Labourt, *Christianisme dans l'Empire Perse*, pp. 288ff.

6. *VIème siécle*, p. 515.

7. Labourt, op. cit., pp. 278, 298.

8. Wright, op. cit., pp. 88–94, citing British Museum Add. 14658.

9. But there is an extract in Italian by Giuseppe Furlani in *Rivesta trimestrale di studi filosofici e religiosi* IV, 1, Perugia 1923. This contains a summary but makes no reference to the *Liber de causis*.

10. E. Gilson, *History of Christian Philosophy in the Middle Ages*, ET, London 1955, p. 182.

11. Wright, op. cit., p. 98.

12. Ibid, pp. 123–4.

13. Ibid., pp. 137–9.

14. *BO* II, Rome 1725, p. 335.

15. Gilson, op. cit., p. 245 for William of Moerbecke.

16. Ibid., p. 434 for his translation of Proclus, finished at Viterbo on 18 May 1268, which exposed the character of the *Liber de Causis* to St Thomas.

17. Ibid., p. 182.

18. Ibid., p. 184.

19. S. H. Nasr, *Science and Civilization in Islam*, Harvard 1968, p. 62.

20. Ibid., p. 44; Wright, op. cit., pp. 211–13.

21. Wright, op. cit., pp. 270–71.

22. See Angus Mackay, *Spain in the Middle Ages*, London 1977, pp. 79–94, especially pp. 81–7 on translation, pp. 88–90 on 'informal acculturation'.

23. See *Quaestiones disputatae de Veritate*, 14 (on faith) 11, reply to the first objection. St Thomas knew of 'wild men in woods', but he had more experience of wise women who practised forms of augury.

24. Summarized by Gilson, op. cit., pp. 222–4.

25. This had been translated into Syriac by Sergius of Reshaina, and its Neo-Platonic sources were known to the Arab world in a variety of ways.

8 *The Impact of the Crusades*

1. See J. Crosland, *Old French Epic*, Oxford 1951, pp. 70–91 on the *Song of Roland*, pp. 208–17 on the earlier *Pelerinage de Charlemagne*.

2. See A. D. Deyermond, *The Middle Ages* in a *Literary History of Spain*, London 1971, pp. 41–7.

3. See *Byz. Pat.*, p. 141 with ref. to MPG 120, col. 147–52.

4. *Byz. Pat.*, p. 88.

5. Ibid., pp. 95, 113–28.

6. In the case of Gregory Asbestas, Metropolitan of Syracuse, who fell out with the Patriarch of Constantinople in 847 and appealed to Rome, the Popes wanted more information, but did not claim immediate jurisdiction. See *Byz. Pat.*., p. 109.

7. He himself was of Italian origin and had been a lawyer before he was a monk.

8. Hildebrand, himself a born Roman, was a supporter of John Gratian, elected as a reformer, Pope Gregory VI, but deposed and exiled with two rival Roman nobles, Benedict IX and Sylvester III, by the German Emperor Henry III at the synod of Sutri in 1046. When Gregory VI died in exile he made the best of it and joined the reformers from beyond the Alps, who at any rate had a vision wider than local Roman politics.

9. It was cited extensively by Humbert of Moyenmoutier, Bishop of Silva Candida, on his embassy to Constantinople in 1054.

10. That he did so at first was made clear by H. Hagenmeyer in an article in *Revue de l'orient Latin* VII, Paris 1899, pp. 324–5, cited in *Byz. Pat.*, p. 161. He retired to Constantinople in disgust when it became clear that Antioch would not be restored to the Byzantine Empire.

11. This material is cited from MPL 143 and MPG 120 in *Byz. Pat.*, pp. 151–2, 187–8.

12. See *Byz. Pat.*, p. 149, citing Leo IX to Michael Cerularius in MPL 143, col. 773–4, and Michael to Peter of Antioch in MPG 120, col. 784.

13. In 1089 the synod of Constantinople required an orthodox 'systatic letter' from the Pope to clarify the position. This was not given.

14. The last Pope in the Byzantine diptychs was John, who could be XVI (997–8), a Calabrian opposed to a German, XVII (1003), who went into a monastery, or XVIII (1003–9). Sergius IV (1009–12) was said to have included the *filioque* in his systatic letter to Sergius II (1000–18), but others said that the breach between them was 'about some sees' or for some unknown reason. Berno of Reichenau in his *Libellus de officio missae*, MPL 142, col. 1060–1, describes the singing of the creed at Rome at the coronation of the Emperor Henry II in 1014 as an innovation. He did not know whether the Roman church continued to sing it, and he said nothing of the *filioque*, which generally went with the tune.

15. See materials assembled by Walter Holtzmann in *BZ* 28 (1928),

pp. 60–64 and cited in *Byz. Pat.*, pp. 156–8.

16. *Byz. Pat.*, p. 167.

17. E.g. in 1107–11, when 'the bishop of the diocess and his clergy' were by 'soft persuasion' and 'furious elocution' pressing the Benedictines of Constantinople not to use *azymes*, unleavened bread, at Mass. A letter of support for them from Bruno of Asti, Abbot of Monte Cassino, is in MPL 165, col. 1085–90.

18. Some of Hugh's writings are in MPL 202. The brothers were responsible for a Latin translation of the Byzantine liturgy.

19. But it is difficult to know in particular cases how much Greek they knew. What is clear is that while some engaged in controversy against 'the errors of the Greeks' others, like William of St Thierry and Richard of St Victor explored the ground common to both sides, and found much of it in St Hilary and St Augustine. See three essays on William of St Thierry in *One yet Two, Monastic Tradition in East and West*, ed., M. Basil Pennington, Kalamazoo, Michigan 1976.

20. Geoffrey Barraclough explains this difference plainly in a paper on *The Medieval Empire*, originally published separately in London in 1950, and republished in *History in a Changing World*, Oxford 1955. The 'Holy Roman Empire' did not begin to be an institution until 1028, and even after that it was still something like a decoration bestowed on Kings of Germany who went on pilgrimage to Rome.

21. Humbert of the Romans, a former Master-General of the Dominican Order, called special attention to the importance of this occasion in his *Opusculum Tripartitum*, prepared for the Council of Lyons in 1274, citing from a paper of Leo Tuscus: 'When in the time of the Emperor Manuel and Pope Alexander III there were negotiations for peace and concord, and nearly everything was settled, the ambassadors of Manuel found Alexander at Venice, where he reconciled Frederick the Great to the Church.' The *Opusculum Tripartitum* is in Peter Crabbe's *Concilia* II, in the school edition, Cologne 1551, pp. 967–1003. I have considered this part of it in an article in *ECR* V, 2 (1973), and cite the passage on p. 40.

22. As Lothair of Saxony did in 1138 for Pope Innocent II to the horror of Cinnamus, the Byzantine historian, expressed in Book 5, c. 7 of his histories, in MPG 133, col. 572.

23. See *Byz. Pat.*, pp. 182–5, and refs.

24. See a *Typikon* ed. E. Kurtz in BZ III (1894), pp. 167, 170, and my own articles on Syrian Christians in Palestine in *ECQ*, VI, 7 (1946) and VII, 2 (1947).

25. A Dzrazadik or 'erroneous Easter' made much trouble in 1102 between the Armenians and 'the inhabitants of Jerusalem', Franks and Syrians.

26. See William of Tyre's account of this in MPL 201, col. 855–6.

27. A Jacobite in controversy with Byzantines could say in MPG 133, col. 297: 'The Latins do not require us to anathematize Severus.'

28. In *BO* II, col. 290–91. The text is in PO XXXI (1965) with an introduction by J. Khoury, who comments on p. 11.

29. *BO* III, col. 514–16, cited in *Byz. Pat.*, p. 67. The other instance shows that Assemani may be over-interpreting.

30. See my article in *ECQ*, VII, 2, and refs. The homage required by the Latin bishops from all the native clergy was 'much more than a political act. It was implicitly an admission of superiority in the Latin rite and the Latin theological tradition.' The Patriarch of Jerusalem said to Burchard of Mount Sion, 'We would willingly live in obedience to the see of Rome and venerate it.' Submission to Latin bishops, after the Crusades, was much more difficult.

31. These demands are summarized in *Byz. Pat.*, p. 174, from letters of Pope Innocent III in MPL 215.

32. Especially in the last chapter of Walafrid strabo, *De Rebus Ecclesiasticis*, MPL 114, col. 963–6.

33. See her *Alexiad* in MPG 131, col. 153 and my comment in *ECQ*, XI (1956), pp. 309–10, and her confused indignation with Pope Gregory VII.

34. Book 5,c.7 in MPG 133, col. 572.

9 *The Holy Places*

1. The Turks had promised before to protect pilgrimages and shrines, but after the Crimean War the state of the Holy Sepulchre became an international question in which Britain and Sardinia were concerned, as well as Russia, Austria and France.

2. The financial balance between them has improved since the Gulbenkian foundation has come to the help of the Armenians, and the Orthodox Patriarchate has turned a good deal of property into profitable hotels.

3. *VIème siécle*, pp. 165–73.

4. So Eutychius of Alexandria in MPG 111, col. 1156.

5. According to his continuator, Yahya of Antioch in PO XVIII, 5, pp. 707–11.

6. A number of pilgrim narratives were translated and published by the Palestine Pilgrim's Text Society in 13 volumes, London 1884–97. Others are *Itinera Hierosolymitana*, Geneva 1879–89, including the *Commemoratorium de casis Dei* made for Charlemagne c. 808 in I, pp. 301–5. See my own article in *ECQ*, VI (1945–6), pp. 363–72.

7. See H. Vincent and F. M. Abel, *Jerusalem*, Paris 1912–26, II, pp. 464ff. They say that the Maronite Patriarch came to spend Easter with them, but this may be a misundestanding of their relation to the Patriarch of Jerusalem.

8. Ibid., p. 896, 'au cours du xivème siécle'.

9. See M. Lequien, *Oriens Christianus* III, Paris 1740, pp. 514–16, Adrian Fortescue, *Uniate Eastern Churches*, London 1923, p. 197, and Donald Attwater, *Catholic Eastern Churches*, London and Millwaukee 1947, pp. 105n, for the difficult history of Roman relations with Jerusalem from the fourteenth century to the sixteenth.

10. Vincent and Abel, op. cit., p. 471.

11. See an article by Charles Frazee on 'the formation of the Armenian Catholic Community in the Ottoman Empire' in *ECR*, VII, 2 (1975).

12. Dositheus, who was patriarch from 1672–1707 and did a great deal for the Church of Jerusalem in such matters as the printing of books and improved educational resources, died at Constantinople, and his successors directed affairs at Jerusalem from the Phanar until 1845.

13. Cited in Frazee, art. cit., p. 156.

14. The use of the word and its derivatives by Arabs and in Swahili caused confusion in the nineteenth century. In Uganda the Franquistas had Catholic connections, but no special association with France. Their political hopes were in Germany. A German is a Frank, whether Catholic or Protestant, but the English had acquired an identity of their own.

15. See Frazee, art. cit., pp. 157–61; M. Ormanian, *The Church of Armenia*, revised edition, London 1955, pp. 71–5.

16. See A. Fortescue, op. cit., pp. 197–202; D. Attwater, *Christian Churches of the East*, I (1947), pp. 105–7, and for comment on the outcome Mgr Joseph Nasrallah in *Istina*, Paris 1976, pp.178ff.

17. See Vincent and Abel, op. cit., 296–8.

18. Accusations that the Greeks rebaptize go back to 1054, and so do Greek criticisms of the Latin ritual of baptism. In practice Greeks have always been much less sensitive than Latins about rebaptizing without an express condition, where there is any uncertainty or defect.

19. See Malachy Ormanian, *The Church of Armenia*, revised edition 1955, pp. 71–5, for an Armenian view of these developments, recorded by Frazee, art. cit., pp. 162–3. Ormanian blames France for the division of the Armenians, but Gallicans had tried to prevent it.

20. The troubled history of this Anglo-Prussian bishopric of Jerusalem was one of the causes of crisis in the Church of England in 1841–5. It was not a success and was finally abandoned after 1879. The Anglican bishopric 'in Jerusalem' is a different foundation, but both grew out of the need of the Western powers to be involved in some way with the Holy Places.

21. See *The Primacy of Peter in the Orthodox Church*, a symposium by Russian authors, originally in French, published in a second English edition in London and New York 1973.

22. But see Philip Sherrard, *Church, Papacy and Schism*, London 1978,

for an orthodox view hostile to any form of primacy.

Appendix – Scholasticism

1. See Vladimir Lossky on 'The procession of the Holy Spirit in the Orthodox Triadology' in *ECQ* VII, 2 (supplementary issue) 1948, and my own on 'Peter Lombard and the Council of Lyons' in *ECR IX* (1977), following up *Misunderstandings between East and West*, pp. 46–9.

Index

131

Index

Index